World Religions

Beliefs Behind Today's Headlines

World Religions

Beliefs Behind Today's Headlines

Buddhism • Christianity • Confucianism
Hinduism • Islam • Judaism
Shintoism • Taoism

A Christopher Book

John T. Catoir
Director, The Christophers

Acknowledgments

Material from "Laotse, the Book of Tao" and "The Emotional and Artistic Life of Confucius" are taken from *The Wisdom of China and India,* edited by Lin Yutang, copyright © 1942 and renewed 1970 by Random House, Inc.; reprinted by permission of the publisher. Excerpts from the *Rig Veda,* translated by Manmutha Dutt, and from the *Talmud,* as translated by Lewis Browne, are taken from *The World's Great Scriptures,* © 1946 by Lewis Browne, and reprinted by permission of The Macmillan Co. The poem entitled "The Neanderthal Man Loved Flowers" is reprinted by permission of its author, Catherine de Vinck.

Cover design by Ann Aspell

Library of Congress Cataloging-in-Publication Data:
Catoir, John T.
     World religions.
     Rev. ed. of: The way people pray. 1974.
     Includes index.
     1. Religions. I. Catoir, John T. Way people pray.
II. Title.
BL80.2.C37   1985   291   85-24921
ISBN O-940518-04-X (pbk.)

Printed in the United States of America

The Christophers
12 E. 48th St.
New York, N. Y. 10017

Table of Contents

God speaks to Man — The Golden Rule — definitions of prayer — influence of prayer — testimonies on prayer — sacred writings — animism — monism — monotheism — polytheism — atheism.

Belief in a Supreme Being — fear of the unknown — tribal liturgies — rites of initiation — symbolism — emergence of polytheism — the power of the word.

Unification of Kingdoms of Upper and Lower Egypt — the pharaoh as supreme ruler — belief in afterlife — Napoleon and Egyptology — faith experience of Egyptians — religion and ethics — animism — Re, God of the Sun — Osiris, ruler of the netherworld — burial ceremonies — religious practices of early Egyptians — concept of Maat — Egyptian priesthood — evolution toward monotheism — Amenhotep IV.

Babylonian origins — the one God — Abraham — the faith of Jews — Hebrew Scriptures — Orthodox, Conservative, Reform — Jewish worship — the Sabbath — Jewish calendar — the Passover — Jewish holidays: Rosh Hashanah, Yom Kippur, Shavuot, Tabernacles, Chanukah.

This book is dedicated to my mother,
may she rest in peace.

PREFACE

The art of plain talk has always fascinated me, but to do it in writing is something that comes only through blood, sweat and tears. This book is the result of five years of clarifying, synopsizing and rewriting. It is offered with love and with the hope that by improving our understanding of one another we can make this a better world.

The Christophers have always been interested in encouraging people of all faiths and no particular faith to work together toward that noble goal. How often we have said, "A better world begins with you."

It may sound naive in this age of big government, big institutions and big business but we know for a fact that one person can make a difference in shaping a better tomorrow for all of us. Our global village is growing smaller and smaller as the technology of communications becomes more refined. People all over the world are made aware of international news events almost as they are happening. There is hardly a corner of the world that can still be called remote. We have access to one another as never before in human history.

Since religious beliefs and practices are such an integral part of every culture, it is important to have a clear idea of the world's major religions. All cooperation begins with mutual acceptance and depends on mutual understanding.

The headlines in our daily papers report news about unknown people in far away places. As often as not, the headlines are negative: "Sikhs Threaten Uprising," "Fundamentalist Muslims in Protest," "Orthodox Jews Clash With Israeli Government." These headlines no more represent the religious realities of the peoples of those lands than headlines about strife in Northern Ireland represent the religious realities of Catholics and Protestants.

Still, the headlines do stimulate questions: Who are these people? What are they like? What do they believe?

All human behavior is related to need and need is often related directly to one's religious convictions. In this age of mass communications, a deeper appreciation of the religious world-view of other peoples will help you understand the world that much better.

It is with this in mind that I present this book to a wider Christopher audience. It is very much in keeping with the spirit of our motto, "It is better to light one candle than to curse the darkness." That motto itself has its roots in another culture that had other beliefs — the Confucianism of ancient China — but it has application for the followers of every belief. It is as universal as the yearning for God that has led to a religious flowering among all peoples.

Father John Catoir
Director, The Christophers

INTRODUCTION

In studying the history of religions and teaching the subject on the college level for four years, I discovered an exciting source of new knowledge which not only deepened my faith in Christ but expanded my appreciation of the sincerity and goodness of other people.

Though we are all different in our approaches to God, there are some startling similarities. The most obvious one is a common belief in the Golden Rule. "Do unto others as you would have them do unto you" is perhaps the most familiar and most basic ethical principle of mankind.

Down through the ages, the human heart has been open to the whispering of exalted aspirations. In spite of the competition for survival, the tyranny of sexuality, the will to power and the violence which has resulted from the dominance of man's lower instincts, the human heart continually rises to sublime ideals. The dissonance and diversity of human experience seems to have one harmonious center from which emanates a power greater than the sum of the obstacles placed in the way of ultimate perfection.

The Golden Rule

The Golden Rule appears in many religions, differently worded but essentially the same in meaning:

Christianity:

All things whatsoever you would that man should

do to you, do you so to them: for this is the law and the prophets. (Matthew 7, 12)

Buddhism:

Hurt not others in ways that you yourself would find hurtful. (Udana-Varga 5, 18)

Confucianism:

Is there one maxim which ought to be acted upon throughout one's whole life? Surely it is the maxim of loving-kindness: Do not unto others what you would not have them do unto you. (Analects 15, 23)

Hinduism:

This is the sum of duty: do naught unto others which would cause you pain if done to you. (Mahabharata 5, 1517)

Islam:

No one of you is a believer until he desires for his brother that which he desires for himself. (Sunnah)

Judaism:

What is hateful to you, do not to your fellowman. That is the entire Law; all the rest is commentary. (Talmud, Shabbat 3id)

Taoism:

Regard your neighbor's gain as your own gain, and your neighbor's loss as your own loss. (Tai Shang Kan Ying P'ien)

Zoroastrianism:

That nature alone is good which refrains from doing unto another whatsoever is not good for itself. (Dadisten-i-dinik, 94, 5)

The development of modern civilization from primitive antiquity has been a gradual climb toward that perfection. Prayer has many definitions, but essentially it is communication with the sublime. By moving away from the noise and confusion of life, man has found within his being a deeper life, a more satisfying level of existence which beckons him to go beyond his immediate sense experience. The voice of God is silent and still, speaking with irresistible sweetness to those who listen.

I wanted to trace the history of this voice, this spirit, to learn about the past from the present. Our parents reflect the characteristics of their great-grandparents, and they in turn reflect their ancestors. Recorded history only dates back about 5,000 years; before that we have only fossils, buried bones and ancient ruins to inform us of man's beginning. Man-like creatures roamed the earth more than two million years ago. The Darwinian hypothesis that man and the modern ape have a common ancestor ties us in some mysterious way to the early primate — whose development took some seventy million years. This vast historical spectrum staggers the imagination.

In spite of the relatively strong appearance of an atheistic influence in the last one hundred years, there is overpowering evidence to suggest that man is a believing creature in touch with his creator; he knows that his destiny exceeds the fleeting years of his temporal life. I wanted to see how prayer influenced the human race, so I went to the archives and found an array of testimonies from some of the world's greatest thinkers.

Testimonies on Prayer

Pray, for all men need the aid of the gods. (Homer, Odyssey, c. 800 B.C.)

Prayer is the greatest of spells, the best healing of all spells. . . . Amongst all remedies this one is the healing one that heals with the Holy Word. (Yasht, Zend-Avesta, c.700 B.C.)

Prayer smites down the strength of all the creatures of Ahriman (the Zoroastrian "devil"). It is the greatest, the best of all spells. (Zend-Avesta, 6th century B.C.)

He who offends against heaven has none to whom he can pray. (Confucius, Analects, c. 5th century B.C.)

An Angel collects all the prayers offered in the synagogues, weaves them into garlands, and puts them on God's head. (Meir, Exod, R., 21, 4, Zohar, Gen., c. 150 A.D.)

If apostles and martyrs, while still in the body, can pray for others, when they ought still to be anxious for themselves, how much more must they do so after they have their crowns and victories and triumphs? (St. Jerome, Attack on Vigilantius, c. 396)

He prays in the temple of God who prays in

the peace of the Church, in the unity of Christ's body; which body of Christ consists of the many in the whole world who believe. (St. Augustine, Ennaration on Psalm CXXX, c. 415)

And why pierceth it heaven, this little short prayer of one syllable (God)? For it is prayer with a full spirit, in the height and breadth of his spirit that prayeth it. (The Cloud of Unknowing, 14th century)

Accursed the life of him in this world who breatheth without uttering the Name. (Guru Nanak, 1496-1538, The Sikh Religion, M. A. Macauliffe)

Granting that we are always in the presence of God, yet it seems to me that those who pray are in his presence in a very different sense; for they, as it were, see that He is looking upon them. (St. Theresa of Avila, Autobiography, 1565)

Prayer is always possible for everyone, rich and poor, noble and simple, strong and weak, healthy and suffering, righteous and sinful. Great is the power of prayer: most of all does it bring the Spirit of God and easiest of all it is to exercise. (St. Seraphim of Sarov, 1759-1833, Conversation with Nicholas Motovilov)

The shorter our allotted time is, the easier it perhaps is to decide to pray for one's enemies. (Soren Kierkegaard, 1813-1855, Meditations from, ed. T. H. Vroxall)

Be not forgetful of prayer. Every time you pray, if your prayer is sincere, there will be new feeling

*and meaning in it, which will give you fresh cour-
age, and you will understand that prayer is an
education. (Feodor Dostoevski, The Brothers
Karamazov, 1880)*

*What a spectacle for heaven and earth is not
the Church in prayer! For centuries without in-
terruption, from midnight to midnight, is repeated
on earth the divine psalmody of the inspired can-
ticles; there is no hour of the day that is not
hallowed by its special liturgy. (Pope Pius XI,
Caritate Christi Compulsi, 1932)*

George Bernard Shaw, the Irish poet and playwright,
once said, "Common people do not pray; they only
beg." And perhaps this has been the greater part of
the story of man's communication with the divine, the
fact that he has so often, so frequently, been a beggar
before his God. All the rituals and incantations of antiquity are related to this begging which is not only
a plea for survival, but a search for meaning.

There has been a longing on the part of man and
a corresponding response from God. In certain areas,
such as the Golden Rule, a common understanding has
emerged, a fundamental unity underlying the diversity of human experience. The longing that rises in the
hearts of people everywhere, in every age, is basically
a longing for security, total security, the desire for a
love that endures, a happiness that will never tarnish.
Survival here and now is certainly man's most immediate preoccupation, but he craves for something
beyond his finite boundaries.

The "good life," *la dolce vita* of the West, does not bring the desired contentment; neither does the regulated life of the socialist state. Health benefits may be available to all, order may be insured by rigid law enforcement, but there is more to happiness than material security. An inner yearning for something beyond is at the heart of man's religious experience. Prayer is as natural to human beings as speech; it is the manifestation of our deepest longing.

But prayer is not the only thing we have in common. We must also contend with misery. We are forced to co-exist with sickness, failure, cruelty and pain. To make sense out of these experiences, not the least of which is death, we must explain them in some way. How can we harmonize the negative elements of existence with our inner longing for greatness, immortality, unending happiness? These are questions human beings have been asking since the beginning. I found the Book of Job in the Jewish bible a good summary of this common human misery.

> *I am brought to nothing; as a wind thou hast taken away my desire: and my prosperity hath passed away like a cloud.*
>
> *And now my soul fadeth within myself, and the days of affliction possess me.*
>
> *In the night my bone is pierced with sorrows; and they that feed upon me do not sleep.*
>
> *With the multitude of them my garment is consumed, and they have girded me about, as with the collar of my coat.*
>
> *I am compared to dirt, and am likened to embers and ashes.*
>
> *I cry to thee, and thou hearest me not: I stand*

up, and thou dost not regard me.

Thou art changed to be cruel toward me, and in the hardness of thy hand thou art against me.

Thou has lifted me up, and set me as it were upon the wind, and thou hast mightily dashed me.

I know that thou wilt deliver me to death, where a house is appointed for everyone that liveth.

But yet thou stretchest not forth thy hand to their consumption: and if they shall fall down thou wilt save.

I wept heretofore for him that was afflicted, and my soul had compassion for the poor.

I expected good things, and evils are come upon me: I wanted for light, and darkness broke out.

My inner parts have boiled without any rest, the days of affliction have prevented me.

I went mourning without indignation; I rose up, and cried in the crowd.

I was the brother of dragons, and companion of ostriches.

My skin is become black upon me, and my bones are dried up with heat.

My harp is turned to mourning, and my organ into the voice of those that weep.

I think it is important to study the history of our religious heritage, not merely to discover beautiful passages from the sacred writings of the world's great religions, but to consider them in context.

The Way People Pray

The way people pray is greatly influenced by the way they view the world. Their understanding of their surroundings has always influenced the way their "nostalgia for paradise" finds its expression.

When men were hunting or fishing for survival, animals played an exaggerated role in their spirit-life. They saw in the beasts a life beyond the visible; conversely, higher beings were often envisioned as animals.

There is a legend passed on from generation to generation among the Haida Indians on the U.S. West Coast. A long time ago, a bear lived in the woods. He was enormous and fierce. When hunger drove him, he would come out and ravage their ancestors' camp. Many were killed, and the braves determined to destroy the beast. They tried everything they knew to lure and trap him, but he always eluded them, outwitted them and by some mysterious intelligence escaped unharmed. For years he survived their best efforts and eventually they came to believe the bear was endowed with a superior spirit. Their fear slowly turned to admiration which, in turn, led them to make peace with their enemy. Incantations to his spirit were sung in the night and ritual dances were designed to imitate his movements in a hymn of praise.

The name "animism" is defined as the belief that nature, and animals in particular, possess individual souls which may exist apart from their material bodies.

When you understand this background, the hymns and rituals of the Haida become charged with a new meaning. Even though we do not share that same limited world-view, we can appreciate the human heart behind these primitive manifestations of worship.

In later centuries when man tilled the soil for his livelihood, other natural objects took on greater significance. The sun, the wind, and the rain, for instance, were personified as divine powers; however, the emphasis on the worship of nature did not necessarily preclude an understanding of one supreme power.

Generally throughout history, human prayer has expressed the same basic longing, the same desire to befriend the superior powers and achieve lasting happiness. Out of this human need a multiplicity of religious traditions and rituals have evolved. This field of study has become so complicated that a separate science has emerged, the science of comparative religions.

I have written this book as an introduction to the religions of the world — with particular emphasis on the importance of prayer in mankind's religious experience. I believe each one of us can grow to appreciate his or her own faith in God by examining how others in their act of believing reach beyond the narrow confines of their individual lives.

The Learning Process

We learn not only from exposition, but also from contrast. What do others seek in life? What were our ancient ancestors like? Did they worship God? Did they believe in an afterlife? Do primitive religions have any similarities with the faith of modern man? What about the ancient religions of the East: Hinduism, Buddhism, Confucianism, Taoism? How do these systems of belief resemble Christianity? How do they differ? What relationship does prehistoric religion have to Judaism? Who was Mohammed, and how did he, a preacher who never performed a miracle, achieve such amazing success in spreading his faith? In what way does Islam relate to the Black Muslim movement in the United States? How did the Shiite Muslims evolve?

These questions will be answered for you as you read on. Some other questions in the study of comparative religions are worth exploring. How do all these religions fit together? How do they relate to one another? How do we make sense out of them all?

Three approaches are possible, but remember that an approach to the question is not necessarily the answer. The approach refers merely to the point of view held by the reader.

(1) You may choose to study comparative religions with a predetermined intent to establish your own faith as preeminent by proving that little significant truth can be found in other religions.

This view seems truncated and foolish when one believes in a good and loving God who in his own way must have manifested something of himself to the millions of people who sought him in past ages.

(2) You may maintain that all religions are basically the same, since they all more or less denounce selfishness and promote the Golden Rule.

But we know there are significant differences between the major religions, and we cannot pretend that they do not exist. The common elements of man's religious history do not obscure the obvious discrepancies. All religious sects stress their own special understanding of the truth; in many cases their conclusions are incompatible. Some will say that Christ was divine; others, that he was merely a great moral teacher, an itinerant rabbi, nothing but a man. These ideas are believed by serious religious-minded people. We cannot say that an idea is correct merely because the believers are sincere. All religions are really and objectively different. And so we come to what you already suspect is my own preference.

3) You may seek to experience other faiths by listening to their teachers and learning from those who have sought the living God down through the ages.

In this approach, you do not close your mind to the striking beauty of truth when it manifests itself in other faiths, nor do you find all religions saying the same thing. You see not only the rich variety of beliefs, but also the mysterious unity underlying the apparent differences. In other words, you grow in understanding.

The major religions of the world urge us to have love for one another by following the Golden Rule, but love implies acceptance. We cannot truly rise to love unless, and until, we strive to understand and accept one another.

The Four World Views

The language, culture and political structure of every human society is profoundly influenced by the particular way in which the people interpret the world in which they live. Every person is a unique composite of many traditions. People do not fit neatly into predetermined slots. Yet it is important for our purposes to distinguish the categories of thought which have evolved in history.

The following breakdown may help to give you an overview of the world's major religions in relation to one another.

I. The monist world-view — all is one

Here, emphasis is placed on the principle of unity underlying the entire universe. God, man, nature and the spirit-world are all seen as elements of one undivided whole. Each visible thing, living or nonliving, animal, vegetable or mineral, is seen as a manifestation of a single invisible world-soul.

This all-pervading world-soul is called "Brahman" by the Hindus. The Hindu law of Karma, which is the basis of the belief in reincarnation, states that everything which now exists emanated from one unit of primeval matter and will be absorbed into it at the end. The word "absorbed" is important here because it implies that individuality is snuffed out when we die. Consequently, for many Asians, individuality exists only in the present life; the "now" counts for very little.

II. The polytheistic world-view — many gods

Polytheists generally pay no heed to any sense of solidarity in creation. Nature-worshipers, the animists, the worshipers of mythical gods, all participate in polytheisic religion.

These people generally live in awe and fear of the spirit-world. They identify many natural events with divine beings and give them names, the god of thunder, the god of rain, etc.

The monist sees God, man and nature as one being; polytheists see man and nature as distinct, while attributing god-like qualities to natural objects. Monotheism on the other hand sees man and nature as distinct, while believing in only one supreme God.

III. The monotheistic world-view — one God

Monotheism is the belief that man and nature were created by one supreme God. Believers in one God can be divided into two categories: the theocratic and the incarnational. A theocratic world-view sees God as exercising full authority over all creation and favoring some creatures over others according to his pleasure. The dominant Father-figure, characteristic of the God of Judaism, is an example of this view. An infinite chasm separates creatures from their creator; God is personal, but totally apart from his creation.

Christianity differs in that it is incarnational. The incarnational world-view has grown out of the theocratic. God has come down to "dwell among us," so that the separation between man and God is bridged. For Christians this entire disjointed universe is reorganized with the being of the Messiah, Jesus Christ. Man and nature are mysteriously reconciled and totally immersed in God.

IV. The atheistic world-view — no God

Atheists see man as supreme in the universe; he can master nature and solve all problems through science and technology. Man, in the last analysis, is his own savior. Agnostics and militant atheists know of no other answer to the riddle of human pain and sorrow. They see no way out beyond death and total extinction. They seek the absolute of freedom within the chaos of absurdity.

It is within the context of these four perspectives that human history has developed and is developing.

The way people pray, if they pray at all, is determined by the way they view themselves and the world in which they live. Even atheists are said to pray in the foxholes of mortal combat.

I hope you enjoy this adventure in learning. I hope it will help you to grow in the love of God and neighbor.

PREHISTORIC RELIGION

Human beings are latecomers to this planet. If you compare Mother Earth to a woman one hundred years old, she would have lived in loneliness — without the company of humans — for over ninety-nine years, eleven months and twelve days. She would have lived with human beings a little more than eighteen days, and with civilized man no more than twenty minutes!

The earth is over four billion years old, but the first truly manlike species appeared only two million years ago. Fish preceded man by nearly four hundred million years, reptiles by two hundred and seventy-five million, dinosaurs by one hundred million. Manlike creatures, not yet human, predated him by more than seventy million years. Civilized man, that unique intelligent species which now dominates the planet, is a newcomer among the living.

How We Know about Prehistoric Times

Through their explorations and diggings, archeologists have learned much about our ancestors from their tools, pottery, carvings and ruins. Such findings serve as clues to prehistoric man, to his way of life and scale of values. Yet, in the absence of recorded history, this information can only be speculative. The first written records appear about 5000 B. C. — which means that for tens of thousands of years before Abraham (1850 B.C.) human societies existed of which we know almost nothing.

How, then, can we understand primitive man's religion? Sherlock Holmes would say, "Elementary, my dear Watson! By deduction."

Every historian knows that today is the consequence of what has gone before, so that existing cultures provide clues about the past which sometimes reveal a complete way of life. Religious historians often begin by studying the mythologies and cultures of primitive people living at the present time: the Pygmies of Zaire or the Aborigines of Australia. By comparing the beliefs, practices and artifacts of such people with the ancient remnants discovered by archeologists, they are able to discern elements common to both cultures. No absolutely accurate conclusion may be drawn, but such comparisons give rise to working hypotheses leading to a deeper understanding of mankind's solidarity.

We know, for instance, that primitive man was as concerned as we with death and the afterlife; elaborate burial rituals demonstrate this dramatically. Food, weapons and the equivalent of money were often buried with the deceased to help him in his new life. Yet, it is useless to try to discover a totally pure and original form of religion.

No religion can be reduced to any one form or structure, although common elements are found in many widely separated cults. Certain beliefs may predominate in certain societies, but never exclusively; different rites, myths and symbols coexist in every religion. That is why it may be misleading to offer precise examples of primitive practices taken out of context, since the emphasis of a tiny part of a tradition might distort the true image of the whole.

Even with the data of archeology, we know little about primitive man. We know that he hunted, ate, feared, loved and died as we do. An appealing expression of this link we have with our primitive ancestors is found in a poem by Catherine de Vinck, called "The Neanderthal Man Liked Flowers":

Words and silences
break into many parts:
   fragments of life, mosaics
not yet completed
   the gaps open like wounds.

The wind comes out of the North,
alive with leaf sounds . . .
Did it, in the beginning, blow dust
at the mouth of the cave, curl
   the smoke of the first fire?
The moon, three-quarter full,
   and silver-drunk,
   slides through chinks in the clouds.
What word was used to speak of the moon?
What small tactile hands built
   a clumsy altar
to honor the god moving distantly
   in the sky?
Long unexplained pauses cut up
the story of man: time spaces
   through which he filtered

to new skills, new shapes, new naming,
   pressed by obscure need
from one stratum to the next,
from one ledge of precarious being
   to another,
   across what gulf, what line of tension,
   holding
   what tenuous thread?

Scars on a hillside, old campfires
   with magic circles of stones, tombs
   deep in the rock, a people
   passing
   in the distance, lost and reborn,
gathering flowers for the dead.

Ancient man no doubt had crude theologies and moral systems with severe taboos. Most prehistoric societies also had liturgies related to hunting, fertility and puberty. Initiation ceremonies and burial rituals were most probably common to all tribes.

These common features found in man's religious history from prehistoric to present times cannot be explained merely by the handing down of customs year after year. There have been tribes and civilizations entirely cut off from the world, isolated from others for centuries by oceans and impassable mountain ranges, and yet their religious beliefs and customs are very similar to those of others halfway around the world with whom they could not possibly have had any contact. Something within man himself seems to produce a constant pattern of religious practices.

The Emergence of Polytheism

Long after the Neanderthal man (c. 180,000 B.C.), primitive men struggled in intellectual darkness. The forces of nature (tornados, floods, earthquakes, scorching sun) were frightening to him either in their own right or as forces animated by some mysterious being. He experienced the forces of nature as personal events, either for the good or for the destruction of his tribe. Since he had no satisfactory explanation of recurring natural calamities, he always felt threatened by unseen powers lurking behind visible reality.

He took steps to make peace with these ominous beings. There was no way he could control the forces themselves, so he called upon his own powers of persuasion to induce these superior beings, as he thought of them, to treat him kindly. Early man was in constant communication with the spirit-world through his mental defensive system expressed through rituals and incantations.

Most of the polytheistic systems had a network of minor dieties; a person could call on the god or gods who had jurisdiction over a specific problem. There was a god for each village, a god for the mountain nearby, a god for the wind and the river; in fact, everything seemed to be animated by the spirits, even the animals. Animism is the name given to this form of primitive worship.

Each spirit had to be propitiated in a special way. Man had to cope with unknown powers and forces, and he created mysterious rituals for that purpose. For instance even today in primitive societies hunters, after killing their larger prey, will disembowel the animal and crawl inside its body to establish good relations with its spirit so that the spirit will not depart the beast and do harm to the hunter later.

Most atheists today trace man's earliest religious instincts to this combined sense of fear and wonder, a condition, they assert, stemming from his own ignorance. But they forget that primitive man had a questioning mind. Something doesn't come from nothing. Throughout the ages, people have asked: "Why am I here? Where am I going?"

If early man was preoccupied with many gods, it does not mean that he was totally ignorant. There is an abundance of evidence to demonstrate that primitive men all over the world carried in their oral traditions a rich heritage and even signs of a knowledge, or distant memory, of one supreme God. After they had exhausted all the avenues of recourse to the minor deities, the God of gods was approached, but only for very important matters. The ordinary affairs of men were too far beneath him.

Most anthropologists today conclude that polytheistic systems are not what they seem. Our primitive ancestors were very much like us. The veneration of the saints today is a barely disguised form of the early reverential instinct. We find Catholics praying to St. Anthony when they have lost their keys because the God on high is too important to be pestered with trivial matters. Hindus, Muslims, Buddhists and Taoists have similar provisions for these petty concerns.

"When the help of all other gods and goddesses has proved disappointing, the Oraon turned to their Supreme Being, Dharmesh: 'We have tried everything, but we still have thee for our helper' " (Mircea Eliade, *Myths, Dreams and Mysteries,* p. 136).

The presence of mythologies with a multiplicity of superior beings does not lead to the denial of an instinctive awareness of one Supreme Being. On the contrary, it seems to support it. This opinion is shared by most religious historians today.

Rite of Initiation

Initiation rites are common to nearly all religions, and our primitive ancestors had elaborate rituals, painfully and meticulously detailed, to achieve a specific purpose. The rites of initiation into puberty are classic examples: they always involve a symbolic death followed by a symbolic resurrection. The revelation of tribal doctrinal secrets to the candidate constitutes the new life, the new experience of the sacred which will characterize his or her admission to adult circles.

Perhaps you saw the movie *Walkabout* where a young Australian aborigine begins the first phase of the ritual. In nearly all initiation rites the mystery begins with a separation from family and tribe, a retreat into the desert or forest. The death symbol is implicit, for the desert or woods represent the "life beyond." The candidate must survive on his own, overcoming personal fear and alien powers.

In the movie, the young aborigine comes upon a teenage girl and her six-year-old brother lost in the desert. The two had traveled for a few days, barely surviving, when across the desert came the lean aborigine with spear in hand and a half dozen lizards hanging on his belt. His face was painted with bright characterisic markings. The plot unfolds and the three become friends. In spite of language and culture differences, the city girl and her brother are guided back to safety. It is a picture of rare quality.

Our interest is in the Australian aborigine. He is on his "walkabout," on his trial in the wilderness, preparing for initiation into the adult male assembly of his tribe. In most tribes throughout the world, there is an initiation hut, tepee, or cave set aside in the bush or desert. Here the young man receives instruction concerning the tribal secrets. The hut symbolizes a womb. The candidate must stay in the fetal state for a determined period of time. His emergence is a symbolic birth, "the dawn of the first day," as the Australian Karadjeri call it.

Some tribes then cover the boy with white powder, in the likeness of a ghost; he must behave as a returned spirit in his ritual dances, gestures and incantations. He is then tortured by the elders to prove he endured the ordeal. His mythical ancestors have symbolically devoured his spirit; it is as though he were digested in the belly of the initiatory monster. Later, a specific ritual operation takes place; in the case of the young male, it is circumcision. A new name is given and the previous life is over, and then the young man is called *Miangu*, which signifies that he is at an advanced stage of the initiation process. Circumcision is not a Jewish invention, as is often believed.

After the walkabout, the tribe anoints the young Karadjeri from head to foot with human blood. Later, his nose is pierced and a quill is passed through the wound. Another ceremony follows, called the *Laribuga*, where the initiate climbs a tree while the men of the tribe sing a sacred song. Usually a climbing rite signifies an entry into the world above, a symbolic ascension into heaven. Many other Australian myths and rituals among the primitive contain these ascension ceremonies.

Still the initiate is not finished. A number of intermediary ceremonies follow until after several years the *Midede* ceremony takes place. The young man is then led by an old man to a secret place where they bury the primal, or ritual poles. The myth of the Bagadjimbiri is then revealed through song and dance. It is their creation myth, a story of two brothers who came up out of the earth in the form of dingos, or wild dogs, which gradually grew to become two human giants. Before the Bagadjimbiri nothing existed at all, neither animal, vegetable nor human and even the ceremony of the buried primals, and the dance itself is said to have been invented by the Bagadjimbiri. The secret of the tribe's origin is revealed.

The initiate's passage from adolescence to manhood, once completed, constitutes the boy's full formal indoctrination into the secrets of the tribe and serves as his formal education, his religious instruction, and his diploma. He learns about his origins, how he came to exist. Nearly all the tribal rituals of the Karadjeri are said to be directly designed by the founding Bagadjimbiri. This creation myth, like countless others, is one example of man's fundamental need to come to terms with his origins. In nearly all creation myths something comes into being from nothing. Something or someone who always was, and who did not need to be created, was responsible for the origins of man. The rich variety of myths from every corner of the world are all designed to explain this mystery.

The Fear of the Unknown

Remember, the Karadjeri are a primitive tribe

living today in Australia. We conclude from evidence found through archeology that primitive men who existed long before recorded history were doing many of the same basic things.

The ancient burial rituals discovered through archeological diggings correspond in many details with the practices of contemporary primitives. We begin to have a feeling for our ancient ancestors; we begin to understand a little the kind of beings they were and how much we have in common with them. Yet we have only scratched the surface. It is very easy for modern man to misread the symbols and come to conclusions which are not accurate; much more must be learned to fill the gaps in our knowledge.

Even today in primitive tribes there are practices which appear to be something other than what they actually are. The contemporary New Zealand aborigine is careful to bury his hair, nail clippings and waste materials. One might think this springs from a desire for cleanliness, but it does not. He is afraid that some hostile person or spirit might come into possession of something that was part of his own body and that enemy would automatically have power to do him physical harm.

The voodoo doll of Haiti is based on a similar principle. By doing harm to a replica of a person, that person is struck by the evil spell. All kinds of incantations and counterattacks are designed to protect against such a travesty. The prayers and music of witches, shamans or medicine men, are designed to allay such fears.

There can be little doubt that our primitive ancestors were crippled with superstitious fears. They treated outsiders as enemies. Their world was a hostile, frightful place.

A good example of this might be found in certain African rituals of exorcism. In the Lango district in North Uganda, an area between five and six thousand square miles, many tribes coexist, though the Lango tribe is the largest, numbering in the neighborhood of a quarter million. The Lango are a Nilotic people, long-limbed, black, lean and muscular. They worship ancestral spirits as well as the one high god they call Jok. No one has ever seen him, and they think of him as the winds. When many deaths occur at once because of disease or pestilence, they attribute it to the path of Jok. Like the air, he is omnipresent. He is the creator of sky and earth and he is generally thought of as benevolent, though given to occasional fits of jealousy. He punishes very severely if he is not properly worshiped. Contemporary African rulers are often inclined to imitate him when they are displeased.

However in his capacity as protector of souls, he is called Jok Orongo. The idea of Jok in the mind of the Lango includes a plurality of spirits unified in the person of a single godhead, a spiritual force composed of innumerable spirits, any of which may be temporarily detached without diminishing the oneness of the force. This includes the souls of certain animals, like giraffes, rhinoceroses, elephants. For some reason lions and leopards are not thought of as possessing souls.

In Jok, a ghost here and there can spring loose. Sometimes a ghost will come back to haunt or annoy his family or his former enemies. A shrine is then built to pacify him. Once in a while a ghost will not be satisfied and will continue to harass the tribe, so it becomes necessary to put him or her to rest once and for all. At this point they summon a medicine man (the *ajoka*, which simply means a man of Jok). He comes and ceremoniously kills a he-goat and smears the blood on the stomach and chest of the person who is haunted by the ghost. He shakes a rattle during this procedure to protect himself, and prepares a small new-made jar with a narrow mouth for the catch. In the jar is placed some food which the deceased ghost is supposed to have liked in his lifetime. The jar is a trap baited to attract the ghost. He calls the ghost by name to come and take his food. The ghost of course is suspicious and begins to ask questions. The *ajoka* tells the ghost he is among friends, all of whom are assembled to watch the expected capture. If any are absent the reason for the absence is explained to the ghost to reassure him. Once secure that everything is up and up, the ghost, who *now* believes he is invited to a family feast, enters the jar to eat the food his soul loves so much.

At once the *ajoka* slams a lid on the jar and fastens it tightly. The jar is carried away and buried in the middle of a swamp. As time passes the stray spirit is once again absorbed into Jok where he belongs, and he no longer threatens the tribe. Sometimes a captured ghost will scream out and threaten to kill them all if they do not let him go. Out of fear they may actually release him provided he promises to be content with his shrine and leave them in peace. If he agrees, they take off the lid and place the jar near his shrine to remind him that he can expect punishment if he is tempted to annoy or harm them in the future.

The Power of the Word

Even today these dark shadows of fear cross the minds of modern men who should know better. If we are more conscious, more sensitive to the dignity of man today, it is because of increased enlightenment. Through the ages we have developed and changed. Our understanding of natural events and our awareness of the proper dimensions of the spiritual have delivered us from many fears which haunted our ancestors. But we must not forget that much of the pseudo-sophistication of contemporary man is a deliberate inadvertence to the mysteries which surround his very existence and destiny, the mysteries of life, death and afterlife.

Rollo May in his book *Love and Will* raises the question, "How does one know that among the bedlam of voices which beset us all, one is really hearing his daimon?" Whether a man goes to his soothsayer, his priest, his psychiatrist, or his counsellor, he is still seeking the answers to his fears, and to the apparent powers that threaten his life. In each instance there are words spoken to him, words which give him an understanding of what is happening to him.

Dr. May says that naming the daimon, personalizing the impersonal, has been and still is the traditional way man overcomes the daimonic. Jesus calls out "Beelzebub!" or "Legion." Exorcists who are successful are able to divine the name of the evil spirit. Today in psychotherapy the therapist seems to succeed in relaxing his patient when he names the evil power which holds him. You have an inferiority complex, or you have extrovert tendencies coupled with repressed hostility toward your mother, or you hate your doctor because of transference, a disguised and suppressed hatred of your father. Words seem to give the patient the sense of penetrating the mystery of his own life, of having received something for his money. "This relief does

seem to have the characteristic of the 'magic' of words,"
says Rollo May.

There is a power in the word, a power given to man,
communicated originally in the form of symbols and
myths; with this power he enters combat with evil and
sickness of soul. Christians believe the word is made
flesh and is still dwelling among us. The power of the
word is total, giving man supremacy over the daimonic
forces in himself and in the world around him.

Man is still in need of protection for survival. We
cannot laugh at our ancestors and their primitive
dances, for we are all in need of light and truth and
the word.

Questions to Think About

1. Were the religions of primitive people based on
fear of the unknown?

2. Would you consider modern Christians, Muslims,
or Jews more enlightened than primitive peoples? If
so, why?

3. Do you, personally, have any superstitious practices? Where did they come from?

EGYPTIAN CIVILIZATION

The Ancient Greeks were young when Egypt was a declining empire. The Greek historian, Herodotus, writing five centuries before Christ, said that Egypt contained "wonders more numerous than those of any other land, and accomplishments so great as to be beyond description." Primitive men were still nestled in caves and huts all over Africa, Asia and parts of Europe when this ancient civilization began to blossom along the banks of the Nile River; it was a culture which grew in richness and splendor, enduring as an empire for more than 2500 years. This unparalleled stability of an entire civilization is in itself one of the great marvels of world history.

The History of Egypt

The earliest Egyptians came to the Nile Valley from somewhere else, we do not know where. They were like the English and French coming to the shores of America, dislodging the primitive inhabitants. It is believed by Egyptologists that 6000 or 7000 years ago these invaders entered from the South, probably from what is today called Somaliland, Africa. Attracted by the Nile's fertile valley, the nomads came and settled, building the marvelous civilization of ancient Egypt.

Villages sprang up rapidly. The surrounding desert discouraged foreign invaders, and a peaceful society developed. The villagers learned to trade with nearby towns, cooperating rather than warring with one another. Eventually they merged and organized themselves to control the Nile's annual flood for mutual protection, so all could benefit from the rich mud deposits left behind when the water receded. Organization on the political level soon followed, and the inherent gift for governing became manifest in the leaders who emerged. Ultimately it was the gift of wisdom in government which explains Egypt's amazing longevity as a state.

By 3500 B.C. the villages had formed two major political entities: the Kingdom of Upper Egypt and the Kingdom of Lower Egypt. Since the Nile flows from south to north, and the earliest settlers entered from the south, the south was called Upper Egypt; Lower Egypt was in the north, toward the Mediterranean Sea. Around 3200 B.C. the great King Menes of Upper Egypt conquered the north, i.e., the delta region of Lower Egypt, and for the first time the two Kingdoms were united under the rule of one: the Kingdom of Upper and Lower Egypt.

It was the world's first real nation under a single monarch, the Pharaoh of Egypt. This succession of pharaohs continued for 30 dynasties. The first two dynasties alone covered almost 400 years. The history of the Nile people is divided into three periods: the Old Kingdom, the Middle Kingdom and the New Kingdom. An Egyptian historian named Manetho recorded this dynastic history around 250 B.C., at a time when Egyptian civilization was slowly waning.

The Old Kingdom lasted from 2700 B.C. to 2200 B.C., the period when the pyramids were built; the Middle Kingdom from 2000 B.C. to 1800 B.C., the period of greatest economic expansion, and the New Kingdom from 1600 B.C. to 1100 B.C. After 1100 B.C. Egypt began its decline, though pharaohs ruled the nation up until the fourth century B.C.

Pharaohs as gods

The pharaoh was the supreme ruler in Egypt. All power was in his hands. He was not only a king, but gradually he became a god. By the 5th dynasty the pharaoh was not just a god, but the incarnate son of Re, the supreme Sun God. As divine monarch, he lived in lush splendor, holding massive power over the lives of millions; it was not difficult for peasants to imagine him as a descendant of Re. The pharaoh was worshiped in temples throughout Egypt and revered everywhere in the kingdom.

It was logical that when a god returned to the afterlife, he deserved a fitting tomb. The pharaohs of the Old Kingdom built the most imposing tombs known to man: the pyramids. In the early period they were buried not only with food, money and jewelry to keep them happy in the next life, but also with the bodies of their servants who were ceremoniously sacrificed to accompany them on their voyage to Re. This practice of human sacrifice was abandoned before the end of the Old Kingdom by a more merciful succession of pharaohs.

Napoleon and Egyptology

Strange as it may seem, Napoleon Bonaparte played an important role in developing the science of Egyptology. In 1798 he travelled there with an army of 38,000 men in 328 ships to conquer the Nile and cut off England's direct route to India. His ambition to conquer Europe depended on striking a fatal blow to the British economy. But his motives were also scientific. He was fascinated by a newly awakened interest in Egyptian culture which was flourishing on the continent at that time, and he organized a team of scholars, botanists, naturalists, historians, linguists and artists to join in the expedition and study Egyptian civilization in detail. About 200 of them were hidden among the soldiers when Napoleon landed on July 2, 1798.

The Turks who then occupied Egyptian territory gave his army very little trouble in their invasion. Soon the French dictator set his scholars to work amassing a vast treasury of historical data, pictures and artifacts. The British were not standing idly by; they knew Napoleon's grand ambition, so a British fleet under Admiral Nelson slipped into the harbor at Abukir and totally destroyed the French ships. Napoleon was stranded with his army in the hot unfamiliar desert terrain.

They had been trapped for many months when Bonaparte decided to sneak out with a hand-picked group of his scientists. He secured a ship and slipped through the British blockade, abandoning his army in October of 1799. By 1801 the British and Turks had destroyed the poor French soldiers left behind, but Napoleon had returned safely to Paris where he published

the results of his findings in a 36-volume work entitled "Description of Egypt." The military expedition was
a disaster, but the scientific discoveries were an enormous success, providing stimulation and information
to archeologists and researchers for decades to come.

The Faith Experience of the Egyptians

Religion was so deeply ingrained in Egyptian life
that human survival was thought to depend on it.
There was no separation of religion, economics and
government as we know it today. Religion was central
to all human activity. The political framework itself
was a theocracy.

Primitive Egyptians were no different from other
primitive people. They had a great respect for the
wonders and mysteries of nature. Animals were held
in awe for their varied abilities and traits. Ferocity in
the lion, strength in the elephant, faithfulness in the
dog, were deified. The first set of Egyptian gods were
characterized as animals. Prior to the pharaohs,
polytheism was standard, animism was as natural to
the Egyptian as the sun rising and setting. A spirit was
seen as the cause of every natural event.

In the early stages of Egyptian life, the jackal, an
animal which is known to dig up human bones, was
the image given to Anubis, the god of the dead. Heavy
stone vaults were common in graveyards precisely to
protect the dead from the hungry jackal. Egyptian art
depicts many of these and other magnificent animal
gods, but as time passed divine images became more
refined.

Re, a local god, was first worshiped in Heliopolis,
a Greek name meaning "The City of the Sun." Re, the

God of the Sun, was the first god to achieve nation-
wide recognition. He reigned supreme for a long while,
but he always had to compete with other minor deities.

Another well-known but lesser Egyptian god was
Osiris, the ruler of the netherworld. Maybe he was a
real ruler whose reputation reached legendary propor-
tions, or a god of fertility, perhaps, left over from
primitive worship, but he is believed to have created
Egyptian civilization. His evil Brother Seth was jeal-
ous of his prominence, so he slew Osiris. But the slain
king was resurrected through the plodding perseverance
of his wife, Isis, who searched for and collected his
dismembered body and pieced the bones together.
Horus, their son, avenged his father's death, slaying
Seth and gaining the right to rule Egypt. It was believed
thereafter that every pharaoh ruled as Horus, and
when he died, he became Osiris. The new pharaoh then
took over to rule on earth as Horus once again, renewing the cycle.

The system of Egyptian deities tends to overlap.
There are many gods, many ideas of creation and also
many different views of afterlife. The Re cult, or solar
cult, believed that the dead pharaoh simply boarded
the sun's heavenly boat to sail across the sky each day.

It may be interesting to review the concept which
ancient Egyptians had of the universe. The world was
envisioned somewhat as a cube. The earth provided
the floor inside the cube, and the mountains on the
edges of the floor held up the sky. The cube was
suspended in space and another sky was underneath
the earth. The sun was thought to go under the earth
and around it at night. The cult of Osiris did not
believe their pharaoh sailed with the sun. When he died
they imagined he passed into the netherworld, or

underside of the earth, to rule below as he once ruled on earth.

In the beginning of the Old Kingdom, the quality of immortality was attributed only to the pharaoh and his family. By the end of this period nobles were included, and they were allowed to have their tombs close to the pharaoh's tombs. It was a kind of sharing of immortality by association.

The changing social structure of Egypt in the Middle Kingdom allowed a more democratic approach to heaven, and ordinary mortals were permitted to enjoy the blessings of afterlife. Magic, rituals, liturgies and sacred rites, once the exclusive property of the pharaohs, became public property and the priestly caste grew in importance. Burial ceremonies were the chief preoccupation of these priests who were in charge of preparing people for the next world. They believed that the afterlife involved a full human existence, not a mere spirit-life. The soul rejoined the body in heaven, and this belief is the basis for the Egyptian practice of mummifying their dead.

It was hoped that by preserving their bodies from decay they would enhance the process of resurrection and provide themselves with a decent start in the new cycle of life. The dry climate was conducive to successful experimentation in the mummification of the dead, but the secrets of this ancient art are still a mystery to us today. The priests who performed it were thought of as acting in the role of Anubis, the god of the dead, who restored Osiris to life after Isis had collected his bones.

The pharaohs were entombed in the pyramids, but paupers were wrapped in a coarse fiber and buried in a communal cemetery. Even the poorest graves

contained food and other articles which would help
the deceased in the next life. There were literally
millions of these graves all along the Nile Valley, but
through the centuries most of them have been looted,
including the great pyramids.

Religion and Ethics

The religion of Egypt had an ethical character as
well. It was believed that a sense of law and order, a
quality called *Maat*, was built into the world by the
gods; it was something like our concept of the natural law, but translated literally it means order, truth,
justice or righteousness. For the Egyptian, *Maat* means
hard work and honest treatment of neighbor.

After the decline of the Old Kingdom, life became
hard and *Maat* became identified with a sense of social
justice. But in the Middle Kingdom prosperity eventually returned and as life became easier, *Maat* was
again seen as a law set down by the gods. That meant
that any dissent about the structure of society or the
power of the pharaohs was forbidden. Reform was un-
thinkable, revolution an impossibility. The gods had
created the world; it was a static world. Everything was
just the way the gods wanted it. Any dissenters who
pitted themselves against the gods and the arms of the
pharaoh were virtually committing suicide.

In this culture the act of creation was seen as one
final piece. There was no Garden of Eden, no period
of past glory, no future age which would be different
or better.

The lifelong concern with death and the elaborate
preparations for it were the major religious preoccupation of the Egyptian. Worship and moral propriety had

their role, of course — one would not expect good treatment from the gods without it — but feathering one's nest, in a material sense, i.e., getting a well-prepared tomb, was a chief concern of Egyptian faith.

Monotheism

The breakthrough from polytheism to monotheism came in the New Kingdom during the reign of Amenhotep IV (1375-1350 B.C.). The people were ordered to renounce all their gods and worship the one true god, Aton. By this time the priestly caste which tended all the shrines of all the gods had grown in power and prestige. Amenhotep struck a blow at their power by exalting Aton as the One God in the universe, the master of life, the creator of all that is. All other gods and their shrines were nullified with one stroke. One of Amenhotep's Hymns to Aton is our earliest record of monotheistic worship.

The dawning is beautiful in the bottom of the sky,
O living Aton, Beginning of Life!
When thou risest in the eastern horizon
Thou fillest every land with thy beauty,
Thou art beautiful, great, glittering,
high above every land.
Thy rays, they encompass the lands, even
all that thou has made.
Thou art Re, and thou carriest them all away
captive
Thou bindest them by thy love.
Though thou art far away, thy rays are upon
earth;

Though thou art on high, thy footprints are the sky.

Thy rising is beautiful, O living Aton, Lord of Eternity;
Thou art shining, beautiful, strong;
Thy love is great and mighty,
Thy rays are cast into every face.
Thy glowing hue brings life to hearts,
When thou hast filled the Two Lands with thy love,
O God who himself fashioned himself,
Maker of every land,
Creator of that which is upon it:
Men, all cattle large and small,
All trees that grow in the soil,
They live when thou dawnest for them.
Thou art the mother and the father of all that thou has made.
As for their eyes, when thou dawnest,
They see by the means of thee.
Thy rays illuminate the whole earth.
And every heart rejoices because of seeing thee,
When thou dawnest as their lord.

The richness of monotheism dominated Egypt for a while but the deeply imbedded polytheistic practices continued to live; a strong devotion to the many other gods still held power over the imaginations of the people. It could be said that Amenhotep IV, by insisting on the worship of one supreme God, paved the way for the worship of Allah in what is now a Muslim Egypt.

Religious Practices of the Early Egyptians

Egypt was monotheistic. Egypt was polytheistic. It was never exactly one or the other. The supreme god was the one god, but the many gods of legend and myth endured in the minds and memories of Egyptians for generations.

No matter what gods a particular priest served in the Middle Kingdom, he had specific rituals to observe. Every morning, for instance, from one end of the Nile Valley to the other, a standard ritual was practiced for centuries. After rising, a group of priests would take a ceremonial bath in their sacred pool. They would clothe themselves in vestments and enter the temple in procession. The public could watch the priests enter the temple courtyard but were not permitted to enter themselves. Inside the temple the chief priest would wait for the first rays of the morning sun and then he would open the sanctuary doors revealing the effigy of the lord god, a mummy-like figure smaller than a man. All priests prostrated themselves and chanted prayers of worship, while the air was clouded with incense to purify the area for the god's appearance. The chief priest would take down the statue, change its garments, perfume it, and set it back in place as the sun rose slowly in approval. Food and drink were provided before the sanctuary doors were closed and sealed with clay until the next morning when the same ceremony was repeated.

There were periodic festivals when the routine was adjusted to allow the common folk a gaze at the effigy. The festival procession through the village where the peasants lined the streets to watch was considered not only a privilege given to the people, but also a day of entertainment for the god. One particular celebration took place in Abydos, the site of the early pharaoh's tombs. Osiris' head is supposed to have been buried there. Throughout Egypt a pilgrimage to Abydos was carried out once a year and those who could afford it made the journey. At this festival the Osiris resurrection myth was reenacted.

The Afterlife for Everyone

The average Egyptian celebrated his own future resurrection. Whereas formerly only the pharaoh was guaranteed immortality, by the Middle Kingdom the ordinary man who was considered a son of pharaoh became worthy of immortality. The following inscription is taken from "Coffin Texts," (I, 197 and translated by R. T. Rundle Clark in *Myth and Symbol in Ancient Egypt*, London, 1960, p. 134). It gives the sense of the common man's self-image in ancient Egypt.

Now are you a king's son, a prince,
As long as your soul exists,
so long will your heart be with you.
Anubis is mindful of you in Busiris,
your soul rejoices in Abydos where your
body is happy on the High Hill.

Your embalmer rejoices in every place.
Ah, truly, you are the chosen one!
You are made whole in this your dignity
which is before me.
Anubis' heart is happy over the work of his hands
and the heart of the Lord of the Divine Hall is
thrilled when he beholds this good god.

*Master of those that have been and Ruler
over those that are to come.*

The priests were always present to implement the
beliefs of their people. In those days the priest shaved
all his hair, including eyebrows and lashes; he lived a
life of monastic purity and dressed in a white loincloth
to set him apart from all other members of society.
Those in full-time service were the only ones allowed
to enter the innermost sanctuary of the temple. Others
of lower rank were specialists of one kind or another:
scholars, musicians, singers or scribes. The latter would
leave their occupations to live in the temple one month
out of four. Women also served as part-time
priestesses, but most women served as singers and
musicians.

The preparation of others for the afterlife was a major duty for the priests. If the deceased was rich, the
burial rite might take as long as 70 days to complete.
A poor man could be wrapped up in about a day and
a half. Salts, spices and resins were mixed in a con-
coction and applied to the dead body in order to preserve it. It would then be swathed in layers of cloth,
varying in quality according to the wealth of the family.
When the preparations were complete, the deceased
was returned to the family for funeral services.

The usual prayers were read and one rather unusual
event took place. It was an "opening of the mouth"
ceremony which was performed as the last rite before
entombment. The body was made ready in this way
to eat, drink and converse with the gods in the next
life. The procession, or parade, to the tomb which
followed has been depicted on countless stone carvings of Egyptian tombs. Burial was always away from

town toward the West where the sun begins its nightly journey under the world. The procession might travel for miles, across the Nile by barge, and on ox-driven carts to the burial site. Ritual chants were sung along the way by bare-headed priests who burned incense to purify the air. The procession would end at the door of the tomb and a final ceremonial dance would be performed as the chant continued. The following prayer is a final preparation for burial.

None Returneth Again
That is Gone Thither

How prosperous is this good prince!
It is a goodly destiny, that the bodies diminish,
Passing away while others remain,
Since the time of the ancestors,
The gods who were aforetime,
Who rest in their pyramids,
Nobles and the glorious departed likewise,
Entombed in their pyramids,
Those who built their (tomb) temples,
Their place is no more.
Behold what is done therein.
I have heard the words of Imhotep and Hardedef,
(Words) greatly celebrated as their utterances.
Behold the places thereof;
Their walls are dismantled,
Their places are no more,
As if they had never been.

None cometh from thence
That he may tell (us) how they fare;
That he may tell (us) of their fortunes,

That he may content our heart,
Until we (too) depart
To the place whether they have gone.

Encourage thy heart to forget it,
Making it pleasant for thee to follow thy desire,
While thou livest.
Put myrrh upon thy head,
And garments on thee of fine linen,
Imbued with marvelous luxuries,
The genuine things of the gods.

Increase yet more thy delights,
And let (not) thy heart languish,
Follow thy desire and thy good,
Fashion thine affairs on earth
After the mandates of thine (own) heart.
(Till) that day of lamentation cometh to thee,
Then the silent-hearted hears not their lamen-
tation,
Nor he that is in the tomb attends the mourning.

Celebrate the glad day,
Be not weary therein,
Lo, no man taketh his goods with him,
Yea, none returneth again that is gone thither.

The asceticism of the Egyptians revolved around the longing in the human breast for a meaning to life which transcends this world. All the religions of the modern world express this same ancient longing.

Questions to think about

1. Why did the Egyptians look upon their rulers as gods? Has this tendency totally disappeared in modern times?

2. What is the connection between believing in a god and believing in an afterlife?

3. Does the fact of death affect your religious beliefs? How so?

JUDAISM

The word "revelation" has profound meaning when contrasted with the ignorance and superstitious fear of primitive man. Many people think of ancient Judaism as the beginning of religious consciousness. The Adam and Eve story in the book of Genesis certainly reports our beginnings, but when one considers it was written around 587 B.C., around the time of the Babylonian exile, it becomes clear that the Judaic-Christian story was written quite a few million years after the fact. Yet, like every creation myth, it carries the same religious teaching: A supreme God created all that is, out of nothing. There is a difference in the Adam and Eve story, and the key to this difference is in the phrase, "And he saw that it was good." Creation is good: flowing from a good God.

Babylonian Origins

We can gain a deeper insight into the beginnings of Judaism by looking more closely into the Babylonian civilization which flourished as far back as 3000 B.C., more than 1000 years before Abraham.

Around 1850 B.C., Abram was the leader of a nomad tribe originating somewhere in ancient Persia.
Abram, as he was called, is the Father of the Jewish
faith. His name was changed to Abraham by God. He
had migrated to Palestine from an ancient culture
which was basically polytheistic, from a people who
believed in many fearsome gods. The significant thing
about Abraham is his total surrender to Yahweh (which
means "I am who am," the name God revealed to
Abraham).

The Babylonians had their own creation myth: man
was created out of the blood of a slain god. Their creation story was an attempt to put order into the incredible disorder of human life. Accordingly, Abraham's
childhood beliefs about creation might very well have
followed the ancient myths of his people, beliefs which
mirrored the turbulence of their own lives. The rivalries
and cunning of men were seen as a reflection of the
power struggles found among the gods.

The chief Baylonian god was Apsu, who was married to Tiamat, a giant female dragon. Ancient Persia
was a land of violent storms and flooding. All the
floods were attributed to the activity of the gods Apsu and Tiamat. These gods had offspring; two of them
were Anu, the lord of the heavens, and Ea, who ruled
over all rainstorms. The son of Ea, who is called Marduk, eventually became the most important of the
deities, because he prevented Tiamat and her illicit lov-
er Kingu from destroying all the gods in an attempt
to seize power. Marduk killed Kingu, and it was from
Kingu's blood that man came into being. He was born
of bad blood. This is the Adam and Eve story of a
major civilization which flourished around 3000 B.C.

The One God

Babylonians believed that man was the corrupt off-spring of an illicit love affair between two power-hungry gods. To them the creator was not good and his offspring was not good. Life for the Babylonians was much like the myth, a struggle filled with blood-shed and violence. It was not difficult for them to ex-plain the mysteries of the universe in these terms.

Abraham no doubt was influenced by these myths which attempted to explain life. No wonder he was stunned by the new understanding of God that was revealed to him. He learned first that there was a su-preme God; and he learned that God was a good God, a personal God, a loving Father. But the most dramatic personal fact for him to learn was that man himself was good and not a vile offspring of some minor dei-ty. He had come from a world where man was a mere plaything for brutal and selfish gods who in their superhuman combat caused the natural disasters which ravished people's lives.

This new understanding of God changed everything for him and for his people. A devotion to Yahweh de-veloped that became the basic character of the Jewish people. The change from polytheistic to monotheistic faith took place within the life of one man, and his new vision has affected countless people for genera-tions down to the present day.

Abraham reacted against a former tradition. His followers gradually abandoned the Babylonian belief that humans are essentially corrupt and depend on the whims of capricious gods. Abraham received a totally new vision of man's relationship with God. Yahweh had mercifully spared Isaac, something a Babylonian god would never do.

An important principle is demonstrated here for, as we shall see time and again in the study of other religions, major changes in religious beliefs come about when great religious leaders react against the existing traditions of their day.

Comparative Religions

Around 500 B.C., Prince Gautama, who became the Buddha, the "Enlightened one," reacted against the interminable cycle of reincarnation and the fatalism of ancient Hinduism. He was a Hindu before he tried to start a new path to God which is now called Buddhism.

Around 620 A.D., Mohammed reacted against the chaos and polytheism of the Arabic world of his times, citing Allah as the one and only God.

Ancient Egypt was perhaps the first world civilization to move from polytheism to monotheism, calling the sun the one true god. Today, Egypt is almost entirely Muslim, following Islam, the religion of Mohammed.

Concerning the devotees of each religion, it is obvious that there is a vast difference between the spirit of the founder and the lives of the followers. The teachings of a master by no means guarantee that his followers do what he asks. For instance, Christ said, "Love your enemies," but Christians seem to have a great deal of trouble just trying to love their friends and relatives. When Mohammed asks a follower to give every year, two-and-a-half percent of his entire wealth to the poor, it does not mean that all Muslims obey. Giving away one-fortieth of all you possess is a considerable act of charity, especially if it is required year in and year out. When the Buddha says that selfish desires must be extinguished before one can truly be called enlightened, it does not follow that all Buddhists are selfless.

The noble intuitions of the founders of the great religions of the world are admirable in their own right, even apart from the degree to which they are integrated into the lives of the devotees of each respective religion. Very few people follow anything or anyone in exactly the same way. Therefore, it is impossible to analyze the nature of each major religious belief on the basis of data received from the current practices of its followers. There are as many Buddhist sects as there are Christian groupings (Protestant, Catholic and Orthodox). All of them are of differing shades, all of them attempting to follow their master in a different manner. The complex process of action and reaction creates divisions and changes, sometimes small, sometimes great. Abraham's reaction to his own past was induced by a process which Jews, Christians and Muslims believe to have been initiated by God. It began by divine revelation.

The Evolution of Judaism

Judaism evolved in three stages. The first stage was under Abraham. As the leader of a nomad tribe he traveled from a land where, in addition to the major deities, each clan had its own god. Abraham's clan was no exception. It was Abraham's total conversion to Yahweh that is the basis of Jewish monotheism.

The second stage of Judaism did not come until 1285 B.C. when Moses established the covenant with Yahweh after the Exodus. The Ten Commandments were given by God to Moses; Abraham's descendants had become a religious nation named after Israel, Abraham's grandson. Israel had twelve sons; each was a father of one of the twelve tribes. It was Moses who inspired a sense of unity to the twelve tribes, and the sons of Israel became one nation.

The third stage of Jewish evolution took place in the activity of prophets who spent their lives and lost their lives still trying to purge their people of the primitive, superstitious and idolatrous instincts which persisted from their polytheistic heritage. Monotheism was not universally practiced even among the followers of Yahweh. In this period the prophets made it more and more emphatic that Yahweh was not merely their national God, but the one and only God, the God of Gods.

The first commandment given to Moses stressed this belief: "I am the Lord your God. You shall not have other gods besides me." This teaching was pounded into the Jewish nation by the prophets Isaias, Jeremias, Job, Joel, Jonas, etc., until no one could misunderstand its meaning: there is only One God; all other worship is idolatry.

Around 1000 B.C., Israel reached a high point in its development. When David conquered Jerusalem, Israel became a kingdom. King David was revered as the crowning blessing of God and the prototype of the Messiah still to come. He was succeeded by King Solomon who built a temple in Jerusalem, but the monarchy soon waned in the face of warring opposition from neighboring tribes.

It is a characteristic of new-formed states that the national god becomes a personification of the power of the state, the way Marduk was for the Babylonians; but Israel was different. The state did not make Yahweh; Yahweh made the state. When the monarchy began to decline, it was seen as Yahweh's punishment, for Yahweh made the kingdom and he alone could break it. The prophets had predicted the nation would dissolve because of its infidelity to Yahweh, and the prophecy proved true.

First the kingdom split in half. Around 721 B.C., the northern half of the kingdom called Sarall, with its capital in Samaria, fell into the hands of the Assyrians, and in 587 B.C. the southern half, called Judah, with Jerusalem as its capital, fell to the Babylonians. Exile and destruction should have snuffed out every vestige of the Jewish faith, but instead there was a faithful remnant which carried on a belief in Yahweh which was more tenacious than ever. Most of those who returned after the exile were from Judah, the southern half of Israel, and the next 500 years of Jewish history are dominated by their slant on the meaning of their religion. Judaism was the name given to the tradition from this point forward.

Tragedy still plagued the Jews. First there was the occupation of their land by the Greeks and later, in 63 B.C., they were invaded by the Romans. Jerusalem and the whole territory surrounding it was a captive of Rome. Judaism endured many persecutions down through the ages and has survived them all.

The Faith of a Jew

There are three elements basic to the Jewish faith:

God, the Torah and the People.

First there is *God* who comes to man to arrange a covenant, a testament or an agreement with his chosen people. Then there is the *Torah*, the first five books of the Bible which constitute the law, but it is more than the law, it is the name given to the total "way of life" which God chooses for his people. God teaches a *pattern of life* which he asks his people to embrace so that he may build them into a community made in his own image and likeness.

The third element is the *People* themselves, a chosen race set apart from others to be formed by God through obedience to his spoken word. Here is the Covenant, the Old Testament. God chooses his people and says, "I will be your God and you will be my people if you accept my Commandments." The people did accept them, and in spite of sporadic infidelity to that commitment, an infidelity challenged over and over again by the prophets, the agreement was sealed.

Every Jew is a descendant of Abraham, the father of the faith, but it was Moses who spoke the words which are repeated by devout Jews every morning and evening of their lives:

> *"Shema Yisroel Adonoi Elohenu, Adonoi, Echod (Hear, O Israel, the Lord our God, the Lord is One)."*

This prayer sharply distinguishes the Jewish faith from all forms of polytheism: God is one, supreme, personal, and interested in his people. Unlike the Hindus and Buddhists, life for the Jews is not an illusion to be overcome or a curse to escape from, but a gift of God, a kingdom prepared for his chosen people, whose rituals and prayers celebrate God's gift of life.

But to be faithful to this good God, one must seek his holy Will. Life must always be lived according to his plan which is contained in the *Torah*: Genesis, Exodus, Leviticus, Numbers and Deuteronomy.

Hebrew Scriptures

The Christian Old Testament (39 books) and the Jewish Bible (24 books) are substantially the same. The order of the books is somewhat different, and Catholics add a few books not found in today's Jewish Bible. Those added were originally collected by the Jewish people who lived in Alexandria, Egypt. The early Christian community was mostly Jewish and it accepted as inspired the texts of the Alexandrian collection. It was not until a hundred years after Jesus' birth that the Jewish rabbis decided which books they would include in what is today's Jewish Bible. However, they counted the books differently.

The first and second books of the Jewish Bible are counted as one; the Twelve Prophets count as only one book, and the books Ezra and Nehemiah count as only one. The Jewish people divide their Bible into three parts.

1) The Torah or The Pentateuch which is made up of the first Five Books of Moses, as mentioned above;

2) The Prophets; and

3) The Writings, which in turn are divided into the Wisdom Literature, the Scrolls, and the Historical Books. It took nearly a thousand years to write the Jewish Bible. The Torah was written as early as 1250 B.C. and the last of the books was completed around 250 B.C.

Over the centuries, the ancient laws and teachings of Moses were added to, modified, strengthened or slackened to suit contemporary circumstances. Most of these changes were part of an oral tradition passed along by the rabbis generation after generation. It was not until six centuries after Christ that this body of tradition and commentary on the Torah was put into written form and called the *Talmud*. It was a compilation of sayings, metaphysical speculations, science, astronomy, history, and legends which became the source of religious inspiration for the many Jews scattered all over the world from Europe throughout the Near East. The Talmud has many beautiful stories which rabbis composed to help explain the law to their people. Here is just one from the Rabbi Simeon ben Yohai who wanted to show that personal sin always has social consequences:

> *"A number of men were seated in a boat and one of them took a drill and began boring a hole beneath him. His comrades exclaimed: 'What are you doing here?'*
>
> *"He replied, 'What concern is it of yours? Am I not boring a hole beneath my own seat?'*
>
> *"They replied, 'Surely it is our business, for the water will swamp the boat and all of us with it.' "*

When the temple in Jerusalem was destroyed, the geographical center of the faith was replaced by the Talmud, a living book of sacred writings. The Diaspora is the name given to the scattered Jews, and the local synagogue became the center of each community's religious life.

Orthodox, Conservative and Reform

Fidelity to the law of the Torah and the prescriptions of the Talmud is central to Jewish piety, but the approach taken to these obligations varies greatly among Jews. For instance, the Sabbath, the day put aside in the Torah for rest and the contemplation of God, is an important day for the Jewish family. The Sabbath has been described as a day on which there is presented a foretaste of the world to come. The day is celebrated with special food, songs, and pious practices.

Orthodox Jews follow the literal interpretation of the sacred books. No secular or mundane activity is allowed on the Sabbath, nor do they engage in any work or travel. They do not pick up the telephone, write letters, go shopping or even touch money on that day. When an Orthodox rabbi conducts services on the Sabbath, he will have to get someone who is not a strict Jew to turn on the lights of the synagogue, open the doors and lock up when everyone has left.

The Conservative Jews relax these strict observances. They remain true to the spirit of the law without feeling the need to go to the extreme of literal observance. Substantially the same ritual is followed, but exceptions are made when sufficient reason presents itself.

The Reform Jew usually ignores the prohibitions of the Sabbath. Many Jews call themselves Reform Jews because they have virtually abandoned all religious practices and yet they do not want to abandon their Jewishness.

Jewish Worship

There is a beautiful quality of praise of God in strict Jewish worship. Prayer practices which date back centuries before Christ include a strong emphasis on the concept of the praise of God. It can be presumed therefore that Jesus recited the same traditional prayer patterns of all good Jews.

For instance, when Jewish people hold a funeral service for their dead, they conclude with the praise of God in a prayer called Kaddish or "sanctification." The Lord's Prayer (Matthew 6:19-15) "Our Father who art in heaven hallowed be Thy name, Thy Kingdom come . . . " resembles somewhat the Kaddish, which starts, "Hallowed and sanctified is Thy great name . . . speedily establish Thy Kingdom of righteousness . . . "

According to Robert Aron, author of *The Jewish Jesus:* "One must understand that in such a setting steeped in religion, the act of blessing is, for Jesus as for any Jew of his time, the key to his relationship to the universe. All events of daily life or natural phenomena are greeted with an appropriate blessing. And this network of blessings is, for each Jew and the whole of Israel, the basis of their participation in the life of the universe and in the unfolding of history."

The principle behind this worship is very simple. All of creation is seen within the sacredness of Yahweh. This sense of the sacred is reaffirmed throughout the life of a good Jew. In communal worship the blessing comes from the whole group. Jewish prayer is unlike Muslim devotion in that it is not an occasion for simultaneous individual private prayer. The whole

Jewish community blesses and praises Almighty God with one voice. This is the Catholic Christian approach as well, the one voice is that of the body of Christ, the Church.

God promised Abraham that he would be given the power to bless, a power which was proper to God alone. "I will bless you and make your name so famous that it will be used as a blessing" (Genesis 12:2). From Abraham the power was transmitted to the priests and prophets and eventually to all the people in their prayer rituals. Everything that is used and enjoyed by men is the occasion of a blessing. It is profane to use God's creation without uttering praise to God in the form of the blessing. The day is filled with opportunities for these prayers. In the morning the religious Jew prayed a blessing which was recited no doubt by Christ himself: *"Blessed art thou, O Lord our God, King of the Universe, who opened the eyes of the blind . . . who settest free them that are bound."*

The morning preparations of washing and dressing are accompanied by the prayer:

> Blessed art thou, O Lord our God, King of the Universe, who has hallowed us by thy commandments, and given us command concerning the washing of the hands.
> Blessed art thou, O Lord our God, King of the Universe, who clothest the naked.
> Blessed art though, O Lord our God, King of the Universe, who bringest forth bread from the earth.
> . . . who createst various kinds of food . . . who gives goodly scent to fruits.

It should not be difficult for the Catholic reader to recognize the prayer at the Offertory of the Mass, a prayer rooted in Jewish tradition:

> *Blessed are you Lord of all Creation, through your goodness we have this bread to offer which earth has given and human hands have formed, it will become for us our spiritual food.*
> *Blessed are you Lord God of all Creation, through your goodness we have this wine to offer, fruit of the vine and work of human hands, it will become our spiritual drink.*

The Jewish ritual is loaded with similar prayers for all occasions: when one receives good news or bad, when one meets a friend, on the occasion of trial or temptation. The most solemn blessing is the one uttered at the synagogue service by the officiating rabbi; it is seen as a blessing of God himself, and this is the solemn moment of the Jewish liturgy.

At a Jewish funeral flowers may ordinarily be sent unless the family has instructed otherwise. Orthodox Jews however do not send flowers. The 23rd Psalm is a favorite scripture reading of many Jewish people at a funeral service. Orthodox and conserative Judaism do not approve of cremation, and discourage embalming out of respect for the body except when civil law requires it. Reform Judaism is less strict. They do not believe in the resurrection of the body, nor the coming of a personal Messiah, but they believe with all other Jews that the actions one performs in life become a living memorial in death. "They still live on earth in the acts of goodness they performed and in the hearts of those who treasure their memory."

The Sabbath

The Sabbath ritual begins at sundown on every Friday. The woman of the house is surrounded by her husband and children as she lights the Sabbath candles with the blessing. "Blessed are thou, O Lord our God, King of the Universe, who has sanctified us by thy laws and commanded us to kindle the Sabbath light." The father then blesses the wine and everyone takes a sip, praising God for the wine which is praised as a "symbol of joy." This ritual begins the twenty-four hour Sabbath period.

The Orthodox Jew will attend synagogue service Friday evening after dinner, Saturday morning for the main liturgy, and again Saturday afternoon. There are almost as many Orthodox Jews as there are Conservative and Reform Jews put together; so while a greater openness and flexibility is present in Jewish worship, the predominant body of the faithful adhere to the strict observance.

The Friday evening service has begun for centuries with the song of the Sabbath, Psalm 92:

> *It is good to give thanks to Yahweh*
> *to play in honour of Your Name, Most High,*
> *to proclaim your love at daybreak*
> *and your faithfulness all through the night*
> *to the music of zither and lyre,*
> *to the rippling of the harp.*
>
> *I am happy, Yahweh, at what you have done;*
> *at your achievements I joyfully exclaim:*
> *"Great are your achievements, Yahweh,*
> *immensely deep your thoughts!"*

Stupid men are not aware of this,
fools can never appreciate it.

The wicked may sprout as thick as weeds
    and every evildoer flourish
    but only to be everlastingly destroyed,
    whereas you are supreme for ever.
    See how your enemies perish,
    how all evil men are routed.

You raise my horn as if I were a wild ox,
    you pour fresh oil on my head;
    I was able to see those who were spying on me,
    so the virtuous flourish like palm trees
    and grow as tall as the cedars of Lebanon.

Planted in the house of Yahweh,
    they will flourish in the courts of our God,
    still bearing fruit in old age,
    still remaining fresh and green,
    to proclaim that the Lord is righteous,
    my rock in whom no fault is to be found!

This is followed by the *Barekhu,* the blessing which
is still the solemn moment of the service. The leader
says: "Bless ye the Lord, who is blessed . . " and the
congregation responds, standing and bowing slightly
in the direction of the table on which the scrolls of
the Law are laid, saying in one voice:

"Blessed be the Lord, who is to be blessed for-
ever and ever."

The Jewish Calendar

The Jewish calendar was originally based on the cycles of the moon. In the lunar calendar each month is twenty-nine and a half days long, the exact period it takes the moon to circle the earth. The Jewish day ends at sunset.

But it takes the earth 365½ days to make a complete revolution around the sun, and as a result, a sun year is about eleven days longer than a moon year.

It wasn't until the Jewish people settled in the land of Canaan that they became farmers and followed the seasons of the sun. They found that lunar time had them celebrating their spring holiday in the cold of winter. So they switched over to the calendar of the sun. They did not, however, measure the year as we do today, by adding one day every four years for a leap year; they added one whole month seven times over a period of nineteen years. As a result some Jewish years have 13 months.

Their calendar is based on the creation narrative in Genesis. The world was created on Rosh Hashanah, New Year's Day. Jewish tradition reckons years from that day, so if you add 3760 to the present year, you will be able to calculate the current Jewish year. All Jews do not interpret the creation story to be literal history, but they all respect the Jewish calendar.

The most important religious days are Rosh Hashanah, Yom Kippur and the Passover. Rosh Hashanah is a two-day holiday celebrated at the start of the Jewish New Year when the shophar is blown. Yom Kippur is the Day of Atonement, a fast day celebrated on the tenth day of the month of Tishri. It is a day for correcting ones wrongdoings. The

Talmud teaches that there are two kinds of wrongdoings (Mishnah Yoma 8.9):
1) that between man and God, and
2) that between humans.

It is understood God has given every person a three-
fold gift: the power to grow physically, intellectually
and emotionally. A person should therefore develop
himself or herself in each category. If one fails to do
so, he offends God, but if he agrees to correct his error, God will grant forgiveness. In relations with others,
however, God expects more. He wants everyone to live
in harmony and will not hear the prayers of those who
hurt others and continue in this wrongdoing.
Therefore, God asks that the guilty one go to the offended party and right the wrong. Then God will hear
his prayers and forgive him. Jesus expressed the same
idea in Matthew 5:23-24.

The Passover

Passover is an annual feast which was instituted to
commemorate the passing over, or sparing of the
Hebrews in Egypt when God smote the first-born of
the Egyptians. The first Passover is described in the
Book of Exodus:

> *And the Lord spoke unto Moses and Aaron
> (Moses' brother) in the land of Egypt, saying: ". . .
> And they shall take of the blood (of the lamb),
> and put it on the two side posts and on the lintel,
> upon the houses wherein they shall eat the flesh
> . . . with bitter herbs they shall eat it . . . and yet
> shall eat in haste — it is the Lord's passover.*
> *"For I will go through the land of Egypt in the*

*night, and will smite all the first-born in the land
of Egypt.*

*". . . I will pass over you . . . and this day shall
be unto you for a memorial, and ye shall keep
it a feast to the Lord . . . for ever."*

The Passover liturgy begins with the *Seder* meal. It
was this meal which became the Last Supper of Jesus
on the night before his passion and death. The meal
itself is an ordinary dinner, with some special foods.
The ritual that accompanies the meal is distinctive,
however, and the sacredness of the occasion is stressed in its commemorative dimension. It begins with a
dialogue when the youngest child asks:

"Why is this night different from all other nights?"

The father replies, "We were slaves unto Pharaoh
in Egypt and the Eternal, Our God, led us from there
with a mighty hand."

The prayers and food requirements are all specified
in the Sacred Scriptures. The *matzoh*, of course, is
unleavened bread which is called the "bread of affliction." It was unleavened bread which was taken in haste
during the flight from Egypt. *Haroset* is a paste made
from apples and nuts and it is remembered as food
used by the Jews while they performed slave-labor for
the Pharaohs.

Jews of strict observance still believe that the
Messiah will one day come, and a glass of wine is put
out at the Seder meal for the Prophet Elijah who will
announce his coming at a Passover meal.

One of the important readings during Passover week
is the memorable passage from the Prophet Ezekiel:

The hand of Yahweh was laid on me, and he carried me away by the spirit of Yahweh and set me down in the middle of a valley, a valley full of bones. He made me walk up and down among them. There were vast quantities of these bones on the ground the whole length of the valley; and they were quite dried up. He said to me, "Son of man, can these bones live?" I said, "You know, Lord Yahweh." He said, "Prophesy over these bones. Say, 'Dry bones, hear the word of Yahweh.' The Lord Yahweh says this to these bones, 'I am now going to make the breath enter you, and you will live and you will learn that I am Yahweh.' "

I prophesied as I had been ordered. While I was prophesying, there was a noise, a sound of clattering; and the bones joined together. I looked, and saw that they were covered with sinews, flesh was growing on them and skin was covering them, but there was no breath in them. He said to me, "Prophesy to the breath; prophesy, son of man. Say to the breath, 'The Lord Yahweh says this; come from the four winds, breath; breathe on these dead; let them live!' " I prophesied as he had ordered me, and the breath entered them; they came to life again and stood up on their feet, a great, an immense army.

Then he said, "Son of man, these bones are the whole House of Israel. They keep saying, 'Our bones are dried up, our hope has gone; we are as good as dead.' So prophesy, say to them, 'The Lord Yahweh says this; I am now going to open your graves; I mean to raise you from your graves, my people, and lead you back to the soil of Israel. And you will know that I am Yahweh,

*when I open your graves and raise you from your
graves, my people. And I shall put my spirit in
you, and you will live; and I shall resettle you on
your own soil; and you will know that I, Yahweh,
have said and done this — it is the Lord Yahweh
who speaks.' " (Ezk. 37: 1-14)*

When God's will is fulfilled for his people, he will
bind together the dead, the fragmented, the disoriented
people of Israel and breathe into them a new life, new
level of being. The promise of a messiah to restore the
kingdom is a promise still enduring in the hearts and
minds of many of the sons of Israel. Among Christians it is believed that the messiah has already appeared in the person of Jesus Christ.

Jewish Holidays

High Holy Days:

Rosh Hashanah. New Year's Day, observed on the
first day of the Hebrew month of Tishri, early
September in the Gregorian calendar.

Yom Kippur. Day of Atonement, observed on the
tenth day of the Hebrew month of Tishri, corresponding to September or early October in the Gregorian
calendar.

Passover or Pesach. This is the holiday of springtime
which commemorates the escape of the Jewish people
from slavery in ancient Egypt. The Seder meal is eaten
at this time. It is observed on the fifteenth day of the
Hebrew month of Nisan, corresponding to the end of
March or early April in the Gregorian calendar.

Pilgrim festivals:

Shavuot or Pentecost. This is the celebration of the late spring harvest and the story of Moses receiving the Ten Commandments on Mt. Sinai:

> *1. I am the Lord your God; you shall not have other Gods before me.*
> *2. You shall not take the name of the Lord, your God, in vain.*
> *3. Keep holy the sabbath day.*
> *4. Honor your father and your mother.*
> *5. You shall not kill.*
> *6. You shall not commit adultery.*
> *7. You shall not steal.*
> *8. You shall not bear dishonest witness against your neighbor.*
> *9. You shall not covet your neighbor's wife.*
> *10. You shall not covet your neighbor's goods.*

The word Pentecost itself is from the Greek meaning "fifty." In the Jewish calendar, Pentecost is fifty days after Passover. (Christians believe that the Holy Spirit descended on the apostles on the Jewish Pentecost, or about fifty days after Jesus' death, which was at Passover time.) The Jewish holiday is observed on the sixth day of the Hebrew month of Sivan, which corresponds to the end of May or early June in the Gregorian calendar.

Tabernacles or Sukkot. This is a feast of joy and thanksgiving celebrated on the fifteenth day of the Hebrew month of Tishri, or October in the Gregorian calendar. A Sukkah is a booth or hut and it refers to the tents in which the Jews lived while wandering in the desert. The most sacred one was where they kept the Torah. It was called the tabernacle. (Catholics use the same term to describe the place where the Holy Eucharist is reserved.)

Victory holidays

Festival of Lights or *Chanukah* (the "C" is silent) is the Jewish holiday of religious freedom. Long ago a Syrian king tried to force all the Jewish people to worship idols. Leaders among the Jewish people, the Maccabees, grew angry and revolted and finally defeated the Syrians after many years of struggle. All idols were then removed from their temple and a great celebration took place. Chanukah commemorates those events and is celebrated on the twenty-fifth day of the Hebrew month of Kislev, which corresponds to a date at the end of November or early December in the Gregorian calendar.

Ethics and Righteousness

In Judaism there is no fixed creed that all Jews must believe in completely. The test of real Jewishness is not intellectual but ethical; it is not how one thinks, but how one lives within himself and with others that counts. Righteousness is the first requirement.

Jewish people do not seek to convert others to Judaism; they have no missionaries. Those who do convert, about 2500 a year in the U.S., do so on their own initiative.

The Catholic Church in the Second Vatican Council denounced a view which many Christians held down through the centuries, namely that the Jews are cursed for their part in the crucifixion of Jesus. The official teaching of the church states explicitly that such an opinion is "out of harmony with the truth of the Gospel and the spirit of Christ."

Questions to think about

1. Devotion to Yahweh is the most powerful force in the unification of the Hebrew people. Does religion still play an important part in the life of Jews?

2. Jesus was a Jew. How did he carry forth Jewish thought in his teaching about righteousness?

3. "All of creation is seen within the sacredness of Yahweh." How does this knowledge affect the life of the pious Jew?

CHRISTIANITY

We are all familiar with the Christmas story: the child in the manger, the young mother, Mary, and her husband, Joseph, seeking shelter in the stable where they were warmed by the breath of beasts; the three wise men who followed a brilliant unusual star and offered the child gold, frankincense and myrrh.

The word "epiphany" is used to commemorate the event of the wise men coming to the child; it means a showing forth, an unveiling. But what the gospel depicted is the revelation not of a powerful king surrounded by a splendid court, nor of any such symbol of power which the world might recognize and respect, but what is shown is a child, a weak, helpless infant in his mother's arms. Christians are asked to look upon this infant, to believe he is the son of God, the very image of God's splendor, to recognize him as the lord of history, the messiah, the savior, the truth, the way, the life.

To the Christian, the wisdom of God contradicts the wisdom of the world and can well be called folly. As St. Paul says, "The foolishness of God is wiser than men and the weakness of God is stronger than men."

The Mystery of the Incarnation

There are many Christian denominations with differing creeds, but they all share a faith in Jesus Christ, the Son of God who came in the person of an infant, born in a small country during a time of oppression. Indeed, it does seem a mysterious folly, one for which there can be no logical explanation, and one for which no one can offer any scientific verification. The happening cannot be categorized or classified; it defies analysis and the laws of logic, yet the world is asked to accept the reality of God crying with an infant's cry, eating, sleeping, growing up and dying a horrible death.

The world is asked to accept the manifestation of God's love, not in abstract terms, but in the full presence of a man in "our image and likeness," one who can weep, suffer, bleed and die. This is the mystery that is shown to the world in the revelation of Jesus Christ, and Christians believe it with awe, love and joy. The child in Mary's arms is the Lord, the Son of God, the one who holds the keys of the kingdom. The message of his coming is that the Father loves us with a love so reckless that he gave mankind not a formula, a philosophy, a symbol to show the way of reconciliation, but he gave his very own son in the person of Jesus Christ.

This is the mystery of the Incarnation.

Christians celebrate and proclaim their faith in this revelation; they accept his lordship over their lives. They imitate the wise men and offer him their gifts, their faith, their gratitude, and their praise for all they have received from his hands. They bring him their joys and sorrows, the lifted chalice of their lives, the gold, incense and myrrh of all their days. They see the world as charged with his splendor, and they understand that their own poor weak and mortal selves are changed and forever blessed because of him, Jesus Christ the messiah.

> *Glory to God in the Highest, and on earth*
> *peace to men of good will. (Lk. 2:13)*

Roman Catholics, the Eastern Orthodox, Quakers, Lutherans and all others who call themselves Christians, believe in the Incarnation, each with their own interpretations.

Cardinal John Henry Newman, the most famous convert to Catholicism in the 19th century, in his *Essays on the Development of Doctrine,* stated that the doctrine of the Incarnation was the leading idea of Christianity. His thesis has become the foundation of the present Constitution of the Roman Catholic Church, a thesis which was formulated and codified at the Second Vatican Council (*Lumen Gentium*).

According to Cardinal Newman, the Incarnation has three aspects: the sacramental, the hierarchical and the ascetical. Every idea in the Church can be reduced to one of these three categories united within the central concept of the Incarnation. God became man, the word was made flesh. In this mystery Christians believe that Christ intends to make his followers into what he is himself, a person united to God the Father for all eternity. This is what it means to rise in Christ, to be divinized, transformed by his love.

Jesus' disciples were convinced of his love for them and for all mankind. "Greater love than this no man hath, than to lay down his life for his friend." The love of God was no longer a divine attribute, or an abstract idea — it was made visible in the person of Jesus Christ.

The Divinity of Christ

Christ's divinity is still a stumbling block for many, as it was even in the beginning. Not until the year 325 A.D., during the Council of Nicea, did the Fathers of the Church face the question of whether Christ was of the same substance as God, or only of similar substance. There were some heretical movements which attempted to mitigate the doctrine. Many of the bishops who participated at that council were old men, lame and disfigured from the persecutions of the Roman Emperor Diocletian. The issue was a vital one for them because they had all testified to its truth at great personal cost. They had seen parents, relatives, friends and brother-priests persecuted and killed for their faith in the divinity of Christ. This was the faith they had inherited from their forefathers. They knew what had been believed from the beginning by thousands upon thousands of Christians. When Diocletian demanded a renunciation of Christ, hundreds of thousands went to their death in a most cruel fashion rather than deny this belief.

The formulation of this dogma was more than an exercise in theology; it was a living act of faithfulness to the word made flesh. The faith of the Church was then sealed in words in the formula of the Nicene Creed. Its doctrinal formulation declaring Christ's true divinity was the product of more than 300 years of costly faith.

This very creed is recited as a profession of faith after the Gospel at Mass in Catholic worship every Sunday, and in many Protestant churches, too.

The Nicene Creed

We believe in one God,
the Father, the Almighty,
maker of heaven and earth,
of all that is seen and unseen.
We believe in one Lord, Jesus Christ,
the only Son of God,
eternally begotten of the Father,
God from God, light from Light,
true God from true God,
begotten, not made, one in Being with the
Father.
Through him all things were made.
For us men and for our salvation he came
down from heaven;
by the power of the Holy Spirit
he was born of the Virgin Mary, and became
man.
For our sake he was crucified under Pontius
Pilate;
he suffered, died, and was buried.
On the third day he rose again in fulfillment
of the Scriptures:
he ascended into heaven
and is seated at the right hand of the Father.
He will come again in glory to judge the living
and the dead,
and his kingdom will have no end.

*We believe in the Holy Spirit, the Lord, the giver
of life,
who proceeds from the Father and the Son.
With the Father and the Son he is worshiped
and glorified.
He has spoken through the prophets.
We believe in one holy catholic and apostolic
Church.
We acknowledge one baptism for the
forgiveness of sins.
We look for the resurrection of the dead, and
the life of the world to come. Amen.*

The Greeks and Roman pagans of the early era of
Christian history were not so much perturbed by the
idea that God could take a human form; after all, this
is how they depicted their own gods. But they were
absolutely startled by the idea that Christians actually believed in a supreme being who was willing to surrender his power and suffer an ignominious death for
mankind. To them such an idea was absurd. But Christians did not believe it was absurd. Too many of them
died for it. They believed that God laid down his life
for them. Their whole faith, life and dedication
became a response to this extraordinary truth. God
became a man like us in all things but sin. All of
human nature, with its weaknesses and proclivity to
evil, was ennobled and dignified by the intimate touch
of the divine presence.

The Faith Experience of Christians

The Christian is one who affirms the reality and
dignity of his own human nature, precisely because of

the reality and dignity of Jesus Christ, the second person of the Trinity, who assumed a human nature. Jesus loved all those who possess such a nature even to the point of giving himself in the only way men can measure total love, by giving himself unto death.

The New Testament has much to offer on the meaning of the Incarnation.

> *He is the image of the invisible God,*
> *the first-born of all creation;*
> *for in him all things were created.*
> *(Col. 1: 15-16)*

> *Though he was in the form of God,*
> *he did not count equality with God*
> *a thing to be grasped,*
> *but emptied himself,*
> *taking the form of a servant*
> *being born in the likeness of men.*
> *(Phil. 2: 6,7)*

> *In the beginning was the Word*
> *and the Word was with God,*
> *and the Word was God.*
> *He was in the beginning with God.*
> *(Jn. 1: 1-2)*

> *All things were made through him,*
> *and without him was not made*
> *anything that was made.*
> *(Jn. 1:3)*

> *All things were created through him*
> *and for him.*
> *(Col. 1:16)*

Once you realize that Jesus is true God and true
man, his message becomes all the more important.
Christ spoke frequently about his mission to announce
the coming of the kingdom. What precisely was his
message?

The words of Jesus

*Then turning to the disciples he said privately,
"Blessed are the eyes which see what you see! For
I tell you that many prophets and kings desired
to see what you see, and did not see it, and to
hear what you hear, and did not hear it." (Lk.
10: 23-24)*

*"Blessed is he who takes no offence at me."
(Mt. 11:6)*

*"The kingdom of heaven is like treasure hid-
den in a field, which a man found and covered
up; then in his joy he goes and sells all that he
has and buys that field." (Mt. 13:44)*

*"The kingdom of heaven is like leaven which
a woman took and hid in three measures of meal,
till it was all leavened." (Mt. 13:33)*

*"The kingdom of heaven is like a grain of mus-
tard seed which a man took and sowed in his
field; it is the smallest of all seeds, but when it
has grown it is the greatest of shrubs and becomes
a tree, so that the birds of the air come and make
nests in its branches." (Mt. 13: 31-32)*

"The kingdom of God is as if a man should scatter seed upon the ground, and should sleep and rise night and day, and the seed should sprout and grow, he knows not how. The earth produces of itself, first the blade, then the ear, then the full grain in the ear. But when the grain is ripe, at once he puts in the sickle, because the harvest has come." (Mk. 4: 26-29)

Jesus — a man of the Father

The New Testament tells how Jesus, the son of God, went on to face hostility, persecution and ultimately death on the cross. Added to the claim of his divinity, the gospels tell of the ignominious reality of his death, an apparent contradiction to many. To understand it, one must understand more about Christ.

The Father was the very center of his life; Jesus had come precisely to do his will. Indeed it was the Father's will that he should undergo the agony and death of a common criminal.

Jesus' prayer was always directed to the Father, his energy was always spent fulfilling the mission given to him by the Father. He prepared for public ministry by going into the desert to pray. He took moments and hours of refuge in isolation from other men to commune with the Father. He prayed to him the night before choosing his apostles. Perhaps the most moving of his prayers came the night before he died when Jesus prayed for his Church. This beautiful plea to the Father, the quintessence of Jesus' prayer, is presented in the Gospel according to John:

"Now, Father, it is time for you to glorify me with that glory I had with you before the world was. I have made your name known to men you took from the world to give to me. They were yours and you gave them to me, and they have kept your word.

"Now at last they know that all you have given me comes indeed from you, for I have given them the teaching you gave to me.

"I pray for them. I am not praying for the world but for those you have given me, because they belong to you: All I have is yours and all you have is mine, and in them I am glorified. I am not in the world any longer but they are in the world and I am coming to you . . . Holy Father . . ." (Jn. 17, 5-11)

Christ calls Almighty God "Father." Literally, "Abba," a word which conveys a far more intimate relationship than our translation. "Abba" in Aramaic is a diminutive form of a familiar address and might be rendered in colloquial English as "Poppa" or "Daddy," the first utterance of a child to his father. It is the same Father whom Jesus taught his followers to address in the Lord's Prayer. Christians are invited by Christ to address the Father with the same childlike abandonment, the same simple dependency. Christ delivered up his life to the Father: "Abba, Abba, into your hands I commend my Spirit."

The Resurrection

In the final scene of the gospel story Jesus is raised by the Father from the dead. From the very beginning of Christianity there was this overwhelming certainty in the community of the faithful that Jesus was resurrected. This conviction was the basis of the Church's early preaching:

> *"If Christ has not been raised, then our preaching is empty and your faith without foundation ... your faith is futile and you are still in your sins." (1 Cor. 15: 14,17)*

There is no scientific evidence of his resurrection, no first-hand witness of the event itself, but the gospels contain accounts of Christ's appearances to Mary, to Peter and the apostles, and then to the larger community of disciples. The themes presented are the same in all the gospel accounts: an empty tomb, the appearance of angels, the presence of a living Christ.

But another miracle easier to grasp is the fact that Christians have died by the hundreds of thousands for this faith, not in a spirit of dejection and resignation, but in joyful triumph which has echoed through the centuries in every Easter celebration, in the celebration of every Catholic Mass and every other worship service in Christendom. This joy is an inexpressible expanse of vision and heart which comes from a knowledge that sins are forgiven; sorrow and pain are wiped away; good triumphs over evil; and that God, the giver of all good gifts, is reckless in his love for man. The crucifix paradoxically is a demonstration of the totality of this love.

Three Persons, One God

Christians believe in one God, but he is described as three distinct persons in one being. The mathematical formula — three equals one — is difficult for any mind to grasp, so it is no wonder that many find it unacceptable. However, Christians have experienced God in their own unique way, and that experience is extremely important in their understanding of the doctrine of the Trinity.

A brief review of the Jewish Bible is needed to understand revelation as it is developed in the New Testament. The ancient Jews spoke poetically of God in many ways, but two dominant themes manifest themselves continually. They knew God could never be understood or visualized, but they made repeated references to his presence as the mysterious "breath of life" and as the spoken "word" at the beginning of creation.

> *"In the beginning God created the earth and sky. Now the world was empty and formless with darkness hanging over deep waters. But the breath of God stirred the waters. God gave the word, 'Let there be light.' And there was light."* (Gen. 1:1-3)

The word was spoken and there was light. The same theme is repeated in the familiar account of the creation of man.

> *"Yahweh shaped man from the clay of the earth and breathed into his nostrils the breath of life, and man became a living being."* Gen. 2:7)

The breath of God was understood as that life-giving power which came from God's very being. His word was understood as power itself, commanding, creating and recreating the universe. God spoke the word through the prophets. Ezechiel's preaching is an example of divine intercession in establishing a new Israel.

> *He said to me, "Son of man, all these bones represent the people of Israel. They have been saying, 'Our bones are dried up, our hope is lost, we have been cut off from our destiny!' " So he told me, "Preach to those bones: You dry bones, hear the word of the Lord! This is what the Lord God says to you bones: I am going to breathe into you and you will live!" (Ez. 11)*

If it was understood that God acted in history through his breath and through his word, it is not difficult to see how the early Christian community began to see a deeper meaning in the words of Christ.

> *"The things I do in my Father's name are my witnesses ... The Father and I are one." (Jn. 10:25)*

> *"But when He, the Spirit of Truth has come, He will teach you all the truth. For he will not speak on his own authority but whatever He will hear He will speak, and the things that are to come He will declare to you." Jn. 16:13)*

Jesus taught by his presence that there was a unity between the word God spoke and the breath he breathed, and a distinction as well. The early Christians began to examine their own experience of God's revelation to them, and they understood Jesus as the word of God:

"And the Word became man and made His home among us." (Jn. 4:14)

The breath of Yahweh was now seen in a similar way, not merely as a divine attribute, an extension of God's power, but as an advocate, a distinct and separate person within the Godhead, descending upon the apostles at Pentecost, filling the Church with new life, renewing the face of the earth.

God's word was experienced personally through, with, and in Jesus. God's breath was experienced in the coming of the Spirit at Pentecost and throughout the history of the Church. The doctrine of the Trinity, one God, but three distinct persons, is a mystery. One either accepts it, or one rejects it.

It may be interesting to note here that for the Hindu, God is described in a variety of ways. He is referred to as "Brahman," and the many faces of Brahman include a trinitarian formula: Brahman the creator, Vishnu the preserver, and Shiva the destroyer. This is a thoroughly different notion of God than that perceived in Christian revelation, but it is nevertheless interesting to see that a religion more ancient than Christianity and Judaism contains an expression of God formulated in terms of a trinity.

Christian Asceticism

All Christians are called by Christ to be perfect. "Be you therefore perfect as also your heavenly Father is perfect" (Matt. 5:48). In considering what he meant by these words we find an extraordinary level of expectation. "Turn the other cheek to one who slaps your face; he who would take away your coat, let him have your cloak also. Love your enemies, do good to them that hate you, and pray for them that persecute and calumniate you" (Matt. 5:44) Christ asked for a degree of perfection seldom found in daily life.

Even in his final prayer at the Last Supper, the first Eucharistic banquet, where he said: "Not for them only do I pray, but for them also who through their word shall believe in me. That they all may be one, as Thou Father in me, and I in Thee . . . that they may be made perfectly one" (Jn. 17: 20, 21, 23) Christ is calling for a perfection in which the soul is assimilated into the life of the Trinity. This was intended for all men, women and children who, through the teachings of the apostles, would believe in Christ through the ages. The love of God is the essence of Christian perfection.

St. Thomas Aquinas put it simply: "The perfection of Christian life consists fundamentally and essentially in charity manifesting itself mainly in the love of God, and, secondarily, in the love of our neighbor."

The summit of Christian perfection to which Christians themselves are called can be reached only in heaven. Only there will the Christian comprehend how small and insignificant his human efforts have been in attaining this sublime goal; only in heaven will we properly understand how much we needed in the way of divine assistance. Nevertheless, there are definite means for attaining holiness, and these are all available to every member of the Church.

The ordinary means of attaining sanctity are prayer, charitable actions, the practice of self-denial, and the sacraments, particularly the Eucharist which for Catholic Christians is Christ's gift of himself under the appearance of bread and wine. These serve to help us in the loving fulfillment of duties in our life. All Christians are thus called to the summit of perfection and all share in the same means to sanctity. There is no difference in the tools used, but certain differences do arise among priests and the laity, monks and nuns, and people of other Christian religions in the way they make use of the ordinary means of spiritual discipline.

Monasticism stresses community life. Those not bound by the religious vows of poverty, chastity and obedience strive for holiness outside of a community framework.

The Christian churches today

This brings up an interesting point.

Ernst Troeltsch in his book *The Social Teaching of the Christian Churches* explained the three approaches taken by Christians down through the ages: withdrawal, immersion and individualism. In the first, the world is viewed as too sinful to influence except at a distance; e.g. the desert fathers who withdrew from it to preserve their purity. The second involves immersion in the world culturally and socially to influence it and change it. The third view is referred to as religious mysticism or individualism. Here the church

is seen merely as the product of a voluntary association of individuals who exist prior to it and cause it
to be.

In 1978 a Gallup poll found that 80 percent of
Americans agreed that an individual should arrive at
his or her own religious beliefs independent of any
churches or synagogues. This kind of thinking has had
a deleterious effect on Christianity. There are now
more than 20,000 separate Christian churches involved in the world ecumenical movement. The number
of such groups increases by more than 170 each year.
The privatization of religion and the promotion of individualism has led to chaos in many cases. Protestants
are generally known to be religious individualists, some
radically so. They put an emphasis on self: "My salvation depends on my decision to accept my Jesus as my
savior, therefore there is no need to connect with any
community."

The Catholic church has taught a different ec-
clesiology from the beginning. God chose a people.
The church is God's creation, a royal priesthood, an
assembly of the elect. The individual is saved through
Jesus Christ, who is forming a kingdom which implies
membership and participation on the part of individuals. The church is seen as the living presence of
Christ, the fundamental sacrament from which all
sacraments are derived. Jesus instituted the church to
minister to individuals for the good of all. Therefore
the Church has both temporal and spiritual priority
over the individual. The Church is by analogy a mother
with authority. She has the right to set standards, challenge conscience and exercise authority. But more, she
is a refuge for sinners, a comforter of the afflicted and

a source of spiritual nourishment on the journey of life.

The Mass

Throughout the two thousand years of Christianity, Catholics have depended for their strength and sustenance on Christ in the Eucharist. The Mass is the highest form of Catholic worship. Public worship, for Catholics, is not a group of individuals gathered in one place for private prayer, like the Muslims. It is the mystical Body of Christ praying. In the liturgy only one voice prays, that of Jesus offering himself to the Father. All those attending unite in him and through him to become one with him in his eternal act of self-oblation. Saints, scholars and sinners and all combinations thereof have been nourished spiritually by this mystery of faith.

The Mass has within it five purposes, or effects:
adoration, *(latreia)*
thanksgiving, *(eucharistia)*
prayer, *(impetratio)*
forgiveness, *(propitiatio)*
and satisfaction for sins *(satisfactio)*.

It is the representation of Christ's death on the cross in ritual form. The body and blood of Christ are offered under the appearance of bread and wine.

There was only one sacrifice for sins, one saving action; Jesus died once and for all, but Catholics celebrate that redemptive act time and again by entering into his surrender to God, the Father. Down through the ages, kings and peasants, presidents and people in all walks of life have attended Mass with devotion, accepting in faith the miracle of Christ's coming in the Eucharist as his way of feeding his lambs and his sheep.

Questions to think about

1. How does belief in the Incarnation affect the way a Christian regards others and himself or herself?

2. Christianity has been described as a religion of paradoxes: discovering life in death, wealth in poverty, strength through weakness, etc. How can this way of looking at things be useful in everyday life?

3. Christian spirituality has been described as the striving for personal perfection. One Gospel story relates Jesus' advice to a young man: "If you would be perfect, go, sell what you possess and give to the poor, and you will have treasure in heaven; and come, follow me" (Matt. 19:21). In your opinion, what is the wisdom underlying this request by Jesus?

ISLAM

A Muslim or Moslem (either form is acceptable) is a follower of Mohammed. The religion of Mohammed is called Islam, not Mohammedanism.

At the turn of the Sixth Century A.D., Mohammed was seen daily ascending Mount Hira, a barren mountain on the outskirts of Mecca. In a small cave he would pray and meditate alone for hours. A momentous struggle was taking place within his soul, a struggle born of spiritual hunger. The world he grew up in was a chaotic one, filled with superstitious fears. Belief in desert spirits and minor deities, called Jinn, abounded. There were a multitude of contentious tribes, each with its own gods, its own language and dress.

For years Mohammed would go to his mountain to pray, returning home each day to his wife Khadija who is remembered for the encouragement she gave him during this long period of soul-searching. It was to Khadija that he first confided his belief that God was speaking to him through the Angel Gabriel. He was to proclaim Allah to the world as the one true God.

The Message of Allah

Mohammed was born about 570 A.D. in Mecca, a city in western Saudi Arabia. His father died before his birth and his mother died before he was seven. He was raised by an uncle, Abu-Talib, who prepared him for a career in business. Traveling in camel caravans loaded with handmade objects from Mecca, Mohammed learned to trade in the foreign markets of Egypt and Palestine. His early travels brought him in contact with Christians and Jews. He became fascinated with their religious heritage. As a young man he was well experienced in the business world and obtained employment as a chief steward for a very rich widow. Though she was fifteen years his senior, he married Khadija when he was 24 years old. Her wealth enabled him to pursue a life of solitude and prayer.

As his mission became increasingly clear, he began to venture into public places and preach the revelations of Allah. In the polytheistic city of Mecca, proclamation of Allah as the only God was a declaration of war on the ancient loyalties of a passionate people. Fierce opposition met him at every turn, not only from the leaders of established religious sects, but also from local businessmen in Mecca who lived off the shrines and pilgrims. To complicate the matter, each shrine proclaimed a local deity. Allah had been known merely as one of the local gods who lived at Mount Hira. For Mohammed to announce the god of Mount Hira as the only God, was to cancel in one stroke the validity of all other shrines. This alone was enough to put his life in danger, but he outfoxed his enemies through an unbelievable series of events which began with his flight from Mecca. The flight, the Hegira, took place in 622 A.D., and is now celebrated annually as a sacred day for Muslims throughout the world. The Hegira is the point in time which Muslims use to reckon the starting point of the Islamic calendar year.

Mohammed escaped to Yathrib, later called Medina, a city about 270 miles north of Mecca. For the first three years he was able to attract only 40 or so followers, but eventually he amassed an army of followers.

Mohammed was honest about his mission. Even when his disciples wanted to make an idol of him, he would resist them:

> *"God has not sent me to work wonders; he has sent me to preach . . . I never said that Allah's treasures are in my hand, that I knew the hidden things or that I was an angel . . . I am only a preacher of God's words."*

But he remembered bitterly those who rejected and spurned him, those who drove him at swordpoint from Mecca, the home of his birth. He began drilling his followers not only in devotion but in zealous aggression. His former policy of friendliness toward the Jews was changed to persecution.

We might better appreciate the meaning of the phenomenal rise of Islam once we understand the struggle of Mohammed against his adversaries. He returned to Mecca with his army and was victorious. From then on he exercised political sovereignty over all Arabia. He abolished idolatry and began forcing Judaism and Christianity to a position of dependency.

He was a revolutionary, not merely on the theological level, but on the economic and racial level as well.

His theory of monotheism called into question all the established religious theories of his day. For generations families had made their living from the shrines attached to the various gods. One temple in Mecca alone had a shrine for every day of the year. He preached loud and clear: "There is only one God, his name is Allah, and I, Mohammed, am his greatest prophet."

In the very beginning he was hesitant and unsure of himself about the idea that God had actually chosen him to preach this message, but his faith grew and his devoted wife reassured him that his private visions were from God. After the death of his first wife, he took new wives for himself, eleven in all.

His military victories made a colossal impact on the Arabs of his day and they saw him as God's chosen warrior. He won adherents to his views all over the Arab world. His movement spread rapidly for a hundred years after his death. Had not the Muslim armies been defeated by Emperor Charles Martel centuries later in the classic battle of Tours, Islam might have become the faith of Europe.

Abraham, the father of Islam

The extent of Abraham's influence in the world of religion is not fully realized by most people. He is not only the father of the Jewish faith and therefore by virtue of Christ's messianic fulfillment of the Old Testament, the father of the Christian faith, but according to Mohammed himself, Abraham is also the father of the Muslim faith.

Mecca is the holy city of Islam. After Mecca and Medina, Jerusalem is Islam's third most important city, but it has the second most important Muslim temple, the Dome of the Rock. This beautiful golden dome is directly above a huge rock which enshrines the spot where Abraham is said to have brought his son Isaac to be sacrificed. This is also the site where Solomon's temple once stood, the same temple to which Christ was dragged the night before he died. The Abraham-Isaac story enshrined in a Muslim temple might surprise a few Jews and Christians, but it is a well-known fact to the followers of Islam.

Abraham came from a land where men were mere playthings of the gods; natural calamities were interpreted as the anger of the gods. To this day we call them acts of God; then they were understood as the revenge of the deities. Abraham was not conditioned as a youth to think of God as kind and loving.

The real significance of God's intervention to spare Isaac was that Abraham learned dramatically for the first time in his life that his God was a God of kindness. Isaac was saved from being sacrificed and God revealed himself as a God of love. This was the most powerful insight into God's personal nature given to man since the beginning of time.

Muslim allegiance to Abraham is based on the same scripture. Mohammed, who began his public ministry nearly 620 years after Christ, was influenced by both the New and the Old Testament in writing the *Koran,* which is the Bible of Islam.

In the Jewish Bible Mohammed read the story of Abraham, his wife, Sara, and his slave girl, Agar. In that story Agar became pregnant by Abraham and, feeling her womanly pride at bearing the offspring of her master, she began to humiliate Sara, who was barren. Sara complained to Abraham about it, and he gave her permission to deal with Agar as she saw fit.

Sara mistreated the slave girl, who eventually ran away. In the wilderness, an angel of the Lord came to Agar and told her to return to Abraham, promising, "I will multiply thy seed exceedingly . . . thou art with child and thou shalt bring forth a son, and thou shalt call his name Ismael, because the Lord has heard thy affliction" (Gen. 16: 10,11)

She did return and gave birth to Ismael who grew up in the presence of Abraham. Eventually Ismael went down to the land of Egypt to settle there, and it is from his offspring that Mohammed and his followers claim direct lineage with Abraham.

What Muslims Believe
The Five Pillars of Faith

The Muslims have much in common with the Judaic-Christian traditions. However, Mohammed claimed that Christ was merely God's servant, a prophet, but not equal to Allah. Mary, who is mentioned respectfully thirty-four times in the Koran, is referred to as the mother of Christ, never the mother of God. The Trinity is rejected:

> *They surely disbelieve who say: "Behold, Allah is the Messiah, son of Mary . . . Allah is the third of the three," when there is no god save the One God. (Koran)*

Mohammed made it very clear that certain things were expected of his followers. There are Five Pillars of the Islam faith, which are five principles given to Mohammed to regulate a Muslim's religious life.

The first pillar has to do with his creed; it is a very

simple creed that is phrased in the following words: "There is no God but Allah, and Mohammed is his prophet." Every Muslim must make this act of faith at least once in a lifetime, but as a practical matter a good Muslim will repeat it many times a day.

The second pillar is prayer. In order to keep his life in close contact with God and be faithful to the Koran which urges him to "be constant" in prayer, he bows low before his maker, expresses his creaturehood and submits himself to the will of God. He does this five times a day, at rising, at noon, in mid-afternoon, after sunset and before retiring. The routine is flexible and subject to adjustment if circumstances demand it. If a traveler is by the roadside at sunset, it is taught in the Koran that Allah's universe is entirely pure and the faithful are to spread their prayer rug anywhere they find themselves at the appointed hour.

In Arab countries it is a common thing to see Muslims wash their feet before prayer to purify themselves, expressing their desire to be worthy and clean in God's sight. Muslims face Mecca when they pray, not only to express their solidarity with their brothers all over the world who are doing the same thing at the same time, but also to revere the Holy City where Mohammed received his revelation and preached the messages of the glories of Allah.

The prayers contain praise, gratitude and petition. There are a variety of prayers; The following set is an example:

> ... *O my Lord, Thou art the Creator. I am only created: Thou art my Sovereign, I am only Thy servant: Thou art the Helper, I am the beseecher: Thou art the Forgiver, I am the sinner: Thou, my*

Lord, art the Merciful, All-Knowing ... O Lord, grant to me the love of Thee. Grant that I may love those that love Thee. Grant that I may do the deeds that win Thy love. Make Thy love to be dearer to me than self, family or than wealth. O Lord: Grant me firmness in faith and direction. Assist me in being grateful to Thee and in adoring Thee in every good way. I ask Thee for an innocent heart, which shall not incline to wickedness. I ask Thee for a true tongue, I pray Thee to defend me from that vice which Thou knowest, and for forgiveness of those faults which Thou knowest. ... for verily Thou art the forgiver of offences and the bestower of blessings on Thy servants.

The third pillar of Islam is the month-long fast. Once a year during the ninth month of the Islamic calendar which is called Ramadan, a strict fast is enjoined. No food or drink, tobacco or sexual intercourse is allowed from sun-up to sunset. For the Arab people, rooted in arid land as they are, this month of fasting is an extraordinary sacrifice. The two principal fast days of the year are the Lesser Festival, the feast of Breaking of the Fast of Ramadan, and the Greater Festival, the Feast of Sacrifice.

At the end of Ramadan a three-day celebration begins with morning prayers, usually out in the open. They pray for good health, good crops, forgiveness of sins and safety from bad luck, as the festival begins. Grudges are forgotten, enemies are reconciled, alms are given to the poor, and the hunger of the long fast is satisfied by three days of eating and rejoicing.

The fourth pillar of Islam is almsgiving. Mohammed required his followers to distribute to the poor each year, two-and-a-half percent of their entire holdings. That means that a Muslim is expected to give away one-fortieth of everything he owns once every twelve months. While it is obvious that all Muslims do not fulfill this prescript to the letter of the law, most of them do. In fact, they usually do it in bits and pieces all year around. The poor share their meager food supply with their neighbors, or give freely of their own labor to help their neighbor in distress.

The fifth pillar of Islam is the pilgrimage to Mecca. If possible this should be made at least once in a lifetime. Elaborate ritual purifications are required before the pilgrim enters Mecca. The men shave their heads and the women cover their heads. No fasting is necessary in Mecca for the pilgrimage, but sexual intercourse and the use of perfume are forbidden. Making the pilgrimage is not an absolute requirement for salvation, but it is a sure sign of fidelity to the will of Allah. Very often the pilgrims are tattoed on their faces and hands to show that they have made the sacred journey.

The biggest celebration of the Muslim year, the Great Festival, is held on the Day of Sacrifice, which is the last day of the pilgrimage to Mecca. Every Muslim all over the world shares in the celebration. It begins with common prayers in the open. The father of the family takes the animal dedicated for sacrifice, a sheep, goat, cow or camel. The head of the animal is turned toward Mecca and it is killed while ritual prayers are recited. One-third of the flesh is given to the poor, one-third to relatives, and one-third is used for the family feast. The festival lasts for three days. This sacrifice commemorates Abraham's willingness to offer his beloved son.

The Koran

The *Koran* (Quran in Arabic, which means "reading") is the Bible of Islam. It has 114 chapters of revelations of Mohammed; each is arranged according to its length, the shortest being the first. The whole text is prefaced by the opening Surah which became the model of Islamic prayer:

Praise be to God, Lord of
  the world;
The Compassionate, the merciful
King on the day of reckoning:
Thee only do we worship, and
  to Thee do we cry for help.
Guide Thou us on the straight
  path, the path of those to whom
Thou has been gracious,
With whom Thou are not angry,
  and who do not stray.

Mohammed claimed that the Angel Gabriel actually wrote the Koran and dictated it to him word for word. His communications with the archangel are supposed to have lasted for a period of about 22 years.

The Sunna is a supplement of the Koran. It contains a collection of traditions, sayings and anecdotes. Both the Koran and the Sunna are reinforced by the principle of Ijma, which states that the beliefs of the majority of Muslims cannot be in error. The Koran, the Sunna and the Ijma are the three source books of Islam.

There are four fundamental beliefs in the Koran:

(a) the world was created by Allah;

(b) man is absolutely subject to the will of Allah in all things;

(c) man must perform the tasks which Allah assigns to him; and

(d) Allah will reward good and punish evil after this life, according to the way man performs his tasks.

These tasks are called the Five Pillars of Islam, which we have just reviewed. A Muslim must perform these five basic duties in life and, if he does, he will have pleased Allah and gained a life of eternal happiness which is depicted in the Koran in human sensual terms.

The Orthodox Muslim takes a fundamentalistic view of the Koran. Every word is considered to be of divine origin. Islam also looks upon the Old and New Testaments of the Judaic-Christian heritage as authentic but incomplete revelations from God. The fullness of revelation is found in the Koran alone as far as they are concerned.

The only miracle attributed to Mohammed is the actual writing of the Koran. He was an uneducated peasant who could hardly sign his own name, yet he produced a book of wisdom that has moved the hearts and minds of millions upon millions of his followers for generations.

The literal interpretation of the Koran often engenders in the Muslim a fierce legalistic spirit. The Koran approves divorce and polygamy, and encourages the use of military power to achieve its goals. The combination of legalism and militarism has often led to violence and bloodshed in the name of Allah.

This doesn't sound very other-worldly, does it? And

yet, it's not so simple to categorize any religion, for each faith has within it currents and counter-currents.

The post-Mohammedan period

Within the first century after Mohammed's death in 632 A.D., there were preachers and ascetics who reacted against the materialism and political power associated with their religion. There were disputes over the "caliph" or successor of Mohammed which led to divisions among the followers. The three most important ones are the Sunnites, the Shiites and the Khawarij.

Christian hermits, contemplatives and celibates all had an impact on Muslim teachers. Though Mohammed denounced celibacy as an abuse of Christ's teachings, by the third century of the Muslim era a group who were identified by their garments of undyed wool *(suf)* began to challenge orthodoxy's hold over the common people. The Sufis, as they were called, eventually introduced liturgical ceremonies and a whole new attitude toward the Koran. Instead of fidelity to the word alone, they taught that direct, personal experience of Allah was possible, so that wisdom comes not only from the Koran, but from Allah's inspiration. By the fifth century the Sufis, whose most praiseworthy leaders were unmarried, were extolling celibacy.

By the eleventh century, the great Al-Ghazali (1058-1111), the Muslim equivalent of St. Augustine, synthesized the whole Sufi movement, paving the way for its acceptance by orthodoxy. To believe that God supplied religious knowledge apart from the Word of God in the Koran gave authority to countless religious practices not enumerated in the Holy Book. Eventually conservative forces regained control of Islam, but to this day Sufism continues to be responsible for a wide diversity of devotions and practices which are truly Islamic but not prescribed by Mohammed.

Islamic prayer

The Koran offers almost nothing regarding the techniques of prayer. Mohammed did direct his followers to face Mecca during the time of prayer, but the positions of the body have developed through tradition. "Perform the prayer at the sinking of the sun to the darkening of the night and the recital of dawn."

Christian baptism has had an influence on the Muslim custom of washing before prayer. Muslims usually begin prayer by washing their feet and spreading a prayer-rug. Many of them stand erect with their hands on each side of their face, palms open with thumbs touching their earlobes.

They then pray, "Allahu Akbar" (which means "God is most great"). The Koran is opened to recite the beginning Surah which we have seen above. Then, bowing from the waist and with hands on knees, they say: "I extol the perfection of my Lord the Great." Standing up again, "Allahu Akbar" is repeated as they slip slowly to a kneeling position from which they bow, touching the ground with the palms and forehead. Rising again to a kneeling position, they sit back on their heels and repeat the profound bow once again, touching the ground with forehead and hands. This is done five or six times while optional prayers are recited. The creed is often repeated during these exercises.

Reliance on warfare

The prayerfulness of the Muslim does not remove him from the harsh realities of human conflict. The following words of Mohammed explain this ambivalence quite clearly:

"Warfare is ordained for you, though it is hateful unto you, but it may happen that you hate a thing which is good for you, and it may happen that you love a thing which is bad for you. Allah knoweth, ye know not . . . Persecution is worse than killing. And they will not cease from fighting against you till they have made you renegades from your religion, if they can. And whoso becometh a renegade and dieth in his disbelief, such are they whose works have fallen both in the world and the Hereafter. Such are rightful owners of the Fire; they will abide therein . . .

"Fight in the way of Allah, against those who fight against you, but do not begin hostilities. Allah loveth no aggressors. And slay them wherever ye find them, and drive them out of the places whence they drove you out . . . If they attack you, then slay them. Such is the reward of disbelievers."

That passage may help you understand the Shiite Muslims, a fundamentalist sect which is spreading rapidly in Arab countries.

Islamic social doctrine

The Muslims sense of justice is vivid not only with respect to enemies, but also in matters of social thought. Without a doubt, Mohammed's social theory hit the tribal civilization of his day with the force of a tornado. His social doctrine broke new ground in three areas: economics, women, and race relations.

Economics: Mohammed tried to instill a social consciousness among the faithful. In his day men and women were victimized by severe poverty and injustice, living under rigid caste systems. Mohammed taught that wealth should be widely distributed and shared with the less fortunate. His device for accomplishing this was basically the fourth pillar of Islam, where one-fortieth of one's income is pledged for redistribution among the poorer elements of society.

Women: There are different opinions about Mohammed's attitude toward women. He is criticized for having a low estimate of women by allowing a plurality of wives. This practice, though degrading to women in our culture, was the common practice for wealthy Arabs. Mohammed did stress the dignity and equality of women in his own way. He rejected the prevalent idea that women were property, that baby daughters were valueless. He forbade infanticide and demanded an equal inheritance for all children. The Koran opens the way for a fuller equality of women and men in education, voting and professional life, though many centuries of the patriarchical domination have dimmed the actual progress of women in most areas of the Arab world.

Mohammed forbade sexual promiscuity outside of marriage and taught men not to abuse women. He sanctified marriage and raised women to a level of dignity that was unknown in the ancient Arabic-speaking world. Remember, this was a world where a father might sell his daughter to the highest bidder; the buyer could then use her as he saw fit.

Race relations: Not only did Mohammed insist upon complete equality among the races, he even encouraged and praised intermarriage as the greatest sign of interracial love and harmony. One of his wives was black, and his own daughter married a black. The Black Muslim movement in the United States is considered heretical by orthodox Islamic teachers precisely because it is racially selective and discriminatory, a stance which Mohammed would condemn as evil.

Questions to think about

1. What ideas do you find attractive in the faith of Islam? What beliefs do you have in common with Muslims?

2. In what way did Mohammed train his followers in forgiveness? Or did he?

3. Can you better understand the attitude of the Iranians today in the light of the Koran's teachings?

HINDUISM

Hinduism, the world's most ancient religion and the third largest of all religions, is really not a religion in the strict sense. In fact, it is more like an amalgamation of three different historical traditions united by a geographical location and a common sacred culture. Hinduism is so named because it is the religion of India, the land around the Indus river, but there are many Hindus also in Burma and Ceylon. Hinduism remained localized in Southern Asia until modern times when the influence of the guru touched the Western world. Hinduism's main theological belief is in one divine and omnipresent being called Brahma.

The Emergence of Hinduism

Hinduism has no historical founder. Its origins reach back to primitive antiquity. Part of the secret of Hinduism's cosmopolitan or syncretic character stems from its evolution since 1500 B.C. Around that time Aryan tribesmen invaded the Punjab from the north. They brought with them their own faith. This was the first of the three traditions which fused with primitive animism.

The spirit of the period is expressed in a collection of hymns called the *Rig Veda*. It is the oldest document of the world's living religions and is made up of animistic songs and prayers personifying nature, attributing divine personalities to the forces of fire, thunder, sunshine, rain, etc. The *Rig Veda* is also a ritual of primitive spells and charms. During this period the religion of India was called Vedaism. Hinduism had not yet evolved.

The *Rig Veda* shows no signs of a belief in reincarnation or caste systems. It is basically the song book of the Ancient Aryans — barbaric, crude and lusty. Gradually, after a period of about 500 years, the Aryans moved from the desert-like Punjab to the valley of the Ganges, where the land was green with lush vegetation. There were three other Vedas (books of knowledge), but they were of less importance.

In five centuries, people change; the sacred writings of the *Vedas* became obsolete and had to be reinterpreted. The archaic language needed updating. The second stage of India's religious development began during this transition period. A class of learned commentators arose, the forerunners of the priestly caste, and they began to write their thoughts and comments on the sacred book.

The Brahmanas (1000-800 B.C.)
The Upanishads (800-600 B.C.)

Two kinds of literature developed: the ritual books called *Brahmanas* and the commentaries called *Upanishad*. The *Brahmanas* made the priestly caste indispensable for salvation, insisting on exact fidelity to the written law. The *Upanishad* stressed the importance of each individual's personal effort in attaining salvation, stressing the need for contemplation and ascetical practices more than dependence on the priests. These works date back to the golden age of India between 1000 B.C. and 500 B.C., and they reveal a movement away from the polytheistic worship of individual dieties to the monotheistic worship of the one who is all, the Brahman.

The Brahman is the central theological idea in both of these later writings. Brahman is the one, unifying, omnipresent God of the universe. Eventually these two literary trends overshadowed the *Rig Veda* and Vedaism gradually became Brahmanism.

Soon after a multiplicity of minor sects began to appear, variations on the theme of Brahmanism. This wide diversity of philosophical offshoots gradually became what we now know as modern Hinduism. Eliot, in his book, *Hinduism and Buddhism,* said that there was no way to describe the incredible complexity of Hinduism, "the same religion enjoins self-mortification and orgies; commands human sacrifices and yet counts it a sin to crush an insect or eat meat; has more priests, rites and images than ancient Egypt or medieval Rome, and yet outdoes Quakers in rejecting all externals."

The *Ramayans* and the *Mahabharata* which contain the well-known *Bhagavad Gita* represent the literature of this period of Hindu development. The Gita (about 1 A.D.) was finally translated into English in 1785 by Charles Wilkins. It is a dramatic poem which raises the question of the propriety of killing people in war.

The Openness of Hinduism

Hinduism differs from Brahmanism in that it is more human and down-to-earth, less esoteric and less inhibited. Brahman is still the all-pervading center, the totality of all that is, but in practice the Hindu is attracted to him under one or another of his manifestations, particularly Vishnu, the savior of man. Vishnu is believed to have walked the earth in human form many times in the history of the world. Because of this, Hindus have no difficulty with the idea of an incarnation and most of them could easily accept Jesus Christ as an authentic incarnation of the Brahman.

The spirit of openness in Hinduism is the key to understanding the tolerance found in this amazing diversity of beliefs. The Hindu accepts every religious sensitivity as coming from Brahman. Since everything is viewed as a passing manifestation of the one underlying unity which is the Brahman, who is the "all," the totality of reality, nothing is really foreign or strange.

When Pope Paul VI made his historic visit to India, the people lined the streets by the hundreds of thousands, and they stood in silence. The pope, though deeply moved, was probably not surprised, for he knew that Hindus regard a high holy man of any religion as a visible and sacred manifestation of the great Brahman. They would not view Catholicism as a false religion, but rather as one of the many expressions of truth which flow from Brahman. Hinduism absorbs everything it considers good.

This is not to say that factionalism is absent from Hinduism — far from it. There are over 845 dialects spoken in India, creating severe communication problems, and there is an elaborate caste system rooted in racial and color differences. The caste system is closely bound up with the law of Karma. This belief in reincarnation looks at each caste as a self-contained unit, a fate determined by birth and not broken until death. Death brings either graduation to a higher state of existence in a new life, or failure and degradation to a lower state. The Untouchable is the lowest human caste, but one can descend to the animal or insect level.

Mother Teresa of Calcutta is a Catholic nun who founded a community of women dedicated to serve the poor and dying. There are 80 million Untouchables in India, and thousands are left to die in the streets of Calcutta. Everyone, including the Untouchables, believes they are only getting what they rightly deserve. Suffering is inevitable, and trying to relieve it is futile. This is the law of Karma. Christian charity opposes this fatalism of India rather dramatically, and the contrast is made obvious in the person of Mother Teresa as she and her followers cart the sick and dying back to their convent hospital each day.

The Faith of a Hindu

Brahman is the ultimate reality. The only definite thing one can say about him is that he is unknowable. For the Hindu any attempt to classify the ultimate one is foolishness. God may or may not be a person, or three persons, or a hundred persons; may or may not be a creator, father or protector. He, she or it is beyond human categorization. The great one is infinite. The unsearchable one will never be known. The ground of being "before whom all words recoil" is mystery, but he is certainly omnipresent.

A rich, almost limitless variety of conceptions have developed concerning God's nature. The Hindu truly believes that Brahman is unknowable, but there are countless sects which describe their God in a highly specific way. Some think of him as a personal God named Saguna Brahman. This image is much like the Christian conceptualization of God: loving, provident, concerned about one and all in every moment of time. Others conceive God as Nirguna Brahman, an aloof, impersonal being. For them, "God isn't dead; he just doesn't want to get involved."

Openness is the key to the diversity of Hindu belief. Every Hindu sees other sects and other religions as expressions of truth; each one sees one of the many faces of Brahman, but no one can see the whole. Each faith is merely an attempt on the part of man to comprehend a particular aspect of God. Thus the Hindu respect for Christianity as an approach is at the same time mixed with a defiant resistance to the idea that any particular religion is the one, true religion.

Missionaries in India

The more enlightened Christian missionaries have for a long time realized that their missionary movement must accomodate itself to the Hindu spirit rather than demand a complete accommodation to one Christian church. Early missionaries from Portugal transplanted Portuguese Christianity to India. Portuguese architecture, customs and modes of piety were presented as the Christian faith. To become a Christian an Indian had to identify with a foreign culture. Obviously there was a low conversion rate in this country, and to this day the Indian government looks with suspicion on all foreign missionaries. On the other hand, missionaries cannot allow their faith to be swallowed up and distorted. This is an on-going tension in most countries with dominant cultures.

The limitless expressions of the great Brahman also include a Hindu trinity. God manifests himself as Brahman, the Creator; Vishnu, the Preserver, and Shiva, the Destroyer, corresponding roughly to the Christian concept of Father, Son, and Holy Spirit. Shiva, the Destroyer, controls all forces which bring living things back to the hidden center or soul of the universe. All living reality one day dies and is then absorbed back into Brahman. This idea of bringing all things back to God is also the idea or mission of the Christian Holy Spirit, although Christians conceive of the Spirit's work as creative rather than destructive.

Hinduism still contains the vestiges of polytheism, which is simply accepted as the many faces of Brahman. India is full of shrines and temples which are inhabited by one or more of the Hindu pantheon of gods. People come to the shrine not for congregational worship so much as to visit the place where their god actually dwells. This is done without denying the undivided reality of Brahman the one world-soul, central to the entire complexus of created reality.

Hindu Prayer Life

Man himself is viewed as an individual expression of the underlying reality of Brahman, the subtle essence, or hidden center of the universe. The totality of creation is conceived as having a single soul which animates every living part. Every living man, woman and child has a unique soul which is called Atman.

Atman is the true self, the hidden self, but it too is more properly a particular expression of Brahman, and therefore though each man's Atman is distinct from every other Atman, it is nevertheless a part of the great Brahman.

The holy men of India teach that man must learn his true nature. Too often men identify themselves with the self they know. This surface self is just a passing reality. Those who fail to search for Atman, their innermost soul, fail to find the face of Brahman within them and miss the real meaning of life. Yoga is an attempt to help man find the supreme reality by finding their own life center.

The ultimate goal of life is the attainment of Nirvana, a state where man escapes from surface preoccupations and illusions by reaching his Atman and thereby attaining union with his deepest God-self. Since all visible reality is held in low esteem, as merely a transitory, irrelevant phase of the life force, the religious Hindu tends to drift further and further away from what we call reality. The only reality is Brahman, the real one, the invisible world-soul.

The Law of Karma

Each life is lived and then it ends. If at the end of life we have discovered the secret and lived according to its law, we will reappear in a new existence with a higher degree of participation in the life of Brahman; this is the concept of reincarnation. The human soul, or Atman, must go somewhere, and it does. It is absorbed into Brahman, and will eventually emerge in a new day to take a new form. What that form will be depends entirely on how well, or how poorly, the individual person gained awareness of his true self.

The law of Karma refers to this cycle of life:

"A man reaps at that age, whether infancy, youth or old age, that which he had sowed in his previous birth. A man gets in life what he is fated to get, and even a god cannot make it otherwise" (Garuba Purana)

Unlike the Christian concept of heaven where we are to rise with body, soul and personality intact, the Hindu heaven is to be annihilated in God. Nirvana means total absorption into the ground of being where individuality is snuffed out and union with God is achieved perfectly, like a drop of water returning to the ocean. Until that state is attained, the Hindu believes he must wander through life, age after age, either in the form of an animal, an insect, a king or a beggar.

Yoga

The discipline designed to help the Hindu achieve his goal in life is called Yoga.

Yoga is based on a theology which teaches two paths or levels of development in approaching God: the Path of Desire and the Path of Renunciation.

The Path of Desire begins with man's craving for pleasure. Hindu faith says go after it, it is good. But eventually the Path of Desire teaches that pleasure is essentially unsatisfying because it is too private, too restricting. It leaves one still hungry for more. The Path of Desire teaches us to leave pleasure as a goal and seek after worldly success. But worldly success is also unsatisfying; it is too competitive and precarious. Since it too centers on self, it is by nature limited, but worst of all it is only a temporary thing, it fades away.

Having lived through these experiences, man should then begin to see the wisdom of a better way: the Path of Renunciation. If the Path of Pleasure could satisfy, the Path of Renunciation would never be needed. But it is needed, and the Path of Renunciation begins with the ideal of service to others. In itself service is superior to all forms of self-interest, but it too is limited and transitory. The individual is limited in his ability to serve others. There is frustration and pain in this path; it lacks the reward of self-awareness. More is desired.

Beyond service, there is within the Path of Renunciation the ultimate Path of Liberation found in contemplation. By touching the infinite center of one's being, man transcends finitude; he contacts divine wisdom, overcomes ignorance, attains the fullness of life and achieves self-realizaton. Futility, boredom and frustration vanish, for union with Brahman is man's final goal. This is the purpose of Yoga, to lead men to liberation.

The Path of Liberation is explored in many ways, and the art of Yoga employs an amazing variety of techniques to attain it. There are four major categories in the practice of Yoga: contemplation, love, work and exercise.

1. Ynana Yoga is intellectual. It aims at self-realization through the use of the mind. It is essentially contemplative. Through knowledge and mental discipline, the yogi concentrates on Brahman, conceived as an impersonal world-soul. The practitioner achieves a union so intense that he no longer feels his own body. To him pleasure and pain are one and the same. He no longer lives in this world. This path is reserved for the few.

2. Bhakiti Yoga is easier to follow. It is union through love. God is envisioned as personal and loving. The yogi directs his love toward God. His goal is union with God himself; he acts for no other motive. God is imagined in various ways. Some think of him as a protector, some as an intimate friend, some as a loving father, and some as a beloved spouse. The ultimate goal is very much like the Christian ideal of perfect charity, where all things are loved because God is loved, and God animates all things.

3. Karma Yoga is for the activist. Union with Brahman is attained through work. Rather than working for worldly success, they work for the glory of God. The Karmi acts as though each thing he does is the last thing he will ever do. The pursuit of perfection in daily work as a means of pleasing God is well-known in Catholic religious communities, but it was practiced in Hinduism centuries before Christ.

4. Hatha Yoga is most familiar in the West. It involves physical exercise of the body. The idea is to discipline the body in such a way as to bring it under total control, thus liberating the mind, freeing it from the distractions of joy and sorrow, pleasure and pain, peace and anxiety. In each case the Yogi seeks the union of Atman-Brahman, and when this is attained he has reached Nirvana.

There is no denying that Hinduism is characterized as an escapist religion. The emphasis is placed on a denial of life and flight from this world. However it would not be accurate to say that Hinduism is coextensive with the practice of Yoga. Yoga is only one aspect of Hindu prayer and religious dedication. To get the feeling of the rich variety of Hindu prayers and beliefs one must review the sacred writings which were briefly outlined in the beginning of this chapter.

Selections from Sacred Writings

The *Rig Veda*, which means "the book of saving knowledge," is the spiritual legacy of a group of barbarian tribesmen from Central Asia. There are more than a thousand psalms contained in it and the following one is addressed to Agni, the god of fire.

> *May Agni, the presenter of oblations, the attainer of success in works, ever truthful, highly illustrious for many noble deeds, divine, come hither with the celestials.*
>
> *Whatever good, O Agni, thou mayest confer upon the giver of oblations that, indeed, O Angiras, belongs to thee.*
>
> *Bowing unto thee mentally, O Agni, we approach thee daily, both morning and evening.*
>
> *Thee, the radiant, the protector of sacrifices unobstructed by Rakahasas, the perpetual illuminator of truth and increasing in thine own room.*
>
> *Like unto a father to his son, O Agni, be easily accessible unto us; be ever present with us for our well-being.*

The following hymn from another book of the *Rig Veda* is ethereal in tone and reveals the same spirit we find in many other sacred writings. Do you see any phrases that remind you of the Jewish Bible?

Bounteous is he who gives unto the beggar who comes to him in want of food and feeble.

Success attends him in the shout of battle. He makes a friend of him in future troubles.

No friend is he who will offer nothing to his friend and comrade who comes imploring food.

Let him depart — no home is that to rest in — and rather seek a stranger to support him.

Let the rich satisfy the poor implorer, and bend his eye upon a longer pathway.

Riches come now to one, now to another, and like the wheels of cars are ever rolling.

The hands are both alike; their labour differs. The yield of sister milchkine is unequal.

Twins even differ in their strength and vigour: two, even kinsmen, differ in their bounty.

The *Upanishads* are the interpretations and commentaries made of the obscure texts of the *Vedas*. The following sacred commentary is from the *Aitareya Upanishad,* and it explores the nature and destiny of the individal soul.

Verily from the beginning he (the Self) is in man as a germ, which is called seed.
This seed, which is strength gathered from all the limbs of the body, he (the man) bears as self in his self (body). When he commits the seed to the woman, then he (the father) causes it to be born. That is his first birth.

That seed becomes the self of the woman, as if one of her own limbs. Therefore it does not injure her.

She nourishes his (her husband's) self (the son) within her. She who nourishes is to be nourished.

The woman bears the germ. He (the father) elevates the child even before the birth, and immediately after.

When he thus elevates the child both before and after his birth, he really elevates his ownself.

For the continuation of these worlds (men), for thus are these worlds continued.

This is his second birth.

He (the son), being his self, is then placed in his stead for the performance of all good works.

But his other self (the father) having done all he has to do, and having reached the full measure of his life, departs.

And departing from hence he is born again. That is his third birth ...

Who is he whom we meditate on as Self? Which is the Self?

That by which we see form, that by which we hear sound, that by which we perceive smells, that by which we utter speech, that by which we distinguish sweet and not sweet, and what comes from the heart and the mind, namely, perception, command, understanding, knowledge, wisdom, seeing, holding, thinking, considering, readiness (or suffering), remembering, conceiving, willing, breathing, loving, desiring?

No, all these are various names only of knowledge (the true Self), consisting of knowledge, is Brahman ... All the five elements, earth, air,

ether, water, fire — these and those which are,
as it were, small and mixed, and seeds of this
kind, and that kind, born from eggs, born from
the womb, born from heat, born from germs,
horses, cows, men, elephants, and whatsoever
breathes, whether walking or flying, and what is
immovable — all that is produced by knowledge
(the Self). Knowledge is its cause.

Knowledge is Brahman.

Sikhism

Sikhism is a little known religion largely confined
to the Punjab region of northwest India. The Sikhs
have become better known in recent times because of
their political struggle with the Indian government.
They are often regarded as a hybrid between Islam and
Hinduism. Some call them Hindus who have simply
assumed the monotheism of the Muslims, but they are
a distinct religious sect.

Their founder Guru Nanak (1469-1539) was born
in Northern India, son of a minor government official.
He studied both Islam and Hinduism, began teaching
a syncretism of both, and was successful. When he
died both groups vied for the possession of his body
and to some extent even today his name is a symbol
of harmony between the two religions.

The Sikhs make their scriptures the central object
of their worship and ritual. The scriptures, called
Granth Sahib, are a collection of writings and sayings
of the ten gurus who succeeded their founder. The
testament of the fifth guru, Arjun (1563-1606), shows
how carefully they disassociated themselves from both

Islam and Hinduism within a century after their founder's death:

> *"I do not keep the Hindu fast, nor the Muslim Ramadan.*
>
> *"I serve him alone who is my refuge.*
>
> *"I serve the one master who is also Allah.*
>
> *"I have broken with the Hindu and the Muslim.*
>
> *"I will not worship with the Hindu, nor, like the Muslim, go to Mecca.*
>
> *I shall serve him and no other for we are neither Hindus nor Mussulmans."*

So fierce was their desire to protect themselves from each group, they developed the art of self-defense as a main component of their faith. Each male Sikh carries the kirpan, or steel dagger, as a symbol of this readiness to resist. They abstain from alcohol, tobacco and refrain from entering into marriage with Muslims. They renounce all penance, celibacy, external religious objects, pilgrimages and the like. For them above all else, religion is prayer and the repetition of the true name of god is the highest form of prayer and the greatest means of salvation. They are pacifist in theory and militaristic in practice and maintain their militarism is only in self-defense. They strive to return to the original teachings of Nanak, who preached love and peace as the highest goal.

Questions to think about

1. Why are Hindus so accepting of the religions of other people?

2. How is Nirvana similar or dissimilar to the Christian concept of heaven?

3. The Hindu urge to de-emphasize the importance of this world in searching for one's innermost soul has been described as "escapist." Do you agree with this evaluation? Why or why not?

BUDDHISM

Buddhism is an outgrowth of Hinduism; the Buddha was reacting against his time as well as certain elements of Hinduism. The two religions, having coexisted in India for nearly 2500 years, are now like two threads woven into a single cloth. Hinduism, the all-pervasive religion of India, has absorbed Buddhism in many places, but both modes of thinking influence the practical life of the average Indian.

The Story of Buddha

About 500 B.C. the Buddha, whose real name was Siddartha Gautama, was born to a wealthy family. His father was a chief, or raga, of the Sakya clan. It is said that in his childhood the young prince was spoiled with golden toys and silk clothing; servants tended to his every wish. He grew to manhood in a closed environment and knew very little of the world outside the palace grounds. One day he wandered outside the gates, and came in contact for the first time with the squalor and misery of the Indian people. He was an extremely sensitive man, and the sight of such suffering sickened him. Depressed and discontented with his own superficial life, he began to reject everything — his riches, his title and the prospect of a comfortable future in the home of his father.

He was passionately alive with a desire to leave home and search out the meaning of his life. Trained in Brahmanism from his earliest years, Siddartha believed in reincarnation and the law of Karma, but these doctrines did not satisfy his thirst for wisdom. The glories of Hinduism left him still hungering for more. Naturally, his first instinct was to search more deeply within the rich traditions of his own religion. Prince Gautama was a newly-married man with a young son when he decided to leave everything. He is said to have exclaimed one night when looking at his small child: "This is a new and strong tie which I have to break." He fled his home, renouncing all his wealth, and joined the Brahmins, the Hindu priestly caste. After long periods of fasting and mortification he found himself to be no wiser, and another heroic decision was made. He left the priesthood and went off again on his own.

After years of searching and near despair, a great event took place in his life. One day, sitting beneath the Bo tree, which means "the tree of wisdom," contemplating life and its meaning, he became aware of an idea which he considered to be the central truth of human life: only by extinguishing all selfish desires can man ever hope to find happiness.

The name "Buddha" means "The Enlightened One" and it is the name Gautama took after his experience under the Bo tree. His fame spread rapidly as he preached his message to thousands of pilgrims who came to hear his revolutionary teachings. He challeng-

ed the Hindu structure of belief by rejecting the whole
unethical system of castes, the dependence for salvation upon paid priests or bribable dieties, and excessive
ceremonials and fatalism. The Buddha taught that no
one need be caught in the inevitable cycle of Karma;
each person could learn to extricate himself from his
suffering by conquering selfish desires.

The Buddha died about 480 B.C., after founding an
order of monks. No one could actually replace him,
so no successor was appointed. For nearly four centuries all his teachings were passed on in an oral tradition. Buddhism was seen as an esoteric sect at first;
its doctrine was designed for the few who had the
wisdom to follow the great teacher, and not for the
masses.

In this way, Buddhism remained just another minor sect of Hinduism until the third century, B.C.,
when a king named Asoka converted and made it the
religion of his state. In its primitive form Buddhism
was called Hinayana; it then evolved and became
known as Mahayana. Language always plays an important role in the development of religion.

Pali was the natural language of Buddha. King
Asoka had the oral tradition of the Hinayana written
in Pali. These books were eventually accepted by the
Buddhists living in Ceylon, Burma and Siam. Another set of scriptures, however, grew up in the Sanskrit
language, and these bore the imprint of influences
from other cultures in the Far East. These were called
the Mahayana Canons. They were less negative and
more worldly than the early Pali Canons, but the Sanskrit scriptures tended to make Buddha into a divine
being, something he himself deplored in his own
lifetime when followers revered him with excessive

devotion. The evolution of Buddhism extends from these early developments right down to the 1970s. We shall consider Zen Buddhism in the following sections.

What Buddhists Believe

The Buddha reacted against the complexity and fatalism of Hinduism. He rejected the cycle of reincarnation as a necessary way to self-realization. He chose a more direct path to Nirvana and taught his disciples that they could ascend the ladder of life through their own efforts without the intervention of the many gods of Hinduism. Buddha denied that there were outside agents helping or hindering man in his search for happiness. He also discarded the caste system. No one was born closer to Nirvana than anyone else; any man, woman or child could find his own happiness by escaping the complexities of Hinduism and concentrating on the elimination of selfish desires.

Five hundred years before Christ, Siddartha Gautama, the Buddha, believed and taught that man created his own heaven and his own hell. The keystone to his religious teachings is called the Four Noble Truths;

1. Man's life is filled with misery and unhappiness. This everyone can plainly see.

2. But this misery and unhappiness is man's own doing; it has been caused by selfish desires.

3. Selfish desires can be eliminated completely, and therefore so can man's unhappiness.

4. There is an eightfold path that leads to the elimination of selfish desire.

The Buddha wanted to help his followers take responsibility for their life and happiness, and not to sit idly waiting for a new life to correct the misery of this one. Suffering exists, and selfish craving is the direct cause of personal suffering. Renounce all selfish desires and be liberated. His way to freedom is expressed in a system, or technique of training, called the eightfold path, which is really nothing more than a form of morality. The eightfold path is a series of correct dispositions and actions which must be mastered. "It is right view (or understanding), right thought (or purpose), right speech, right conduct, right means of livelihood (or vocation), right effort, right alertness (or mind-control), and right meditation."

Each step depends on the completion of the former. The path is merely a means to the end, Nirvana; it is a stripping away of avarice, ambition, lust and all the other vices, in favor of selfless love. You will notice that Buddha does not concentrate on God or the worship of God. This is one reason why Eastern religions are often called "man-centered" rather than "God-centered." Nevertheless the goal of all this searching is Nirvana — union with the ultimate reality.

There have been many schools and sects within Buddhism, each striving to be a chastening simplification of the many possibilities within Hinduism. Buddha rejected the idea of an authoritative caste which had infused, or special, knowledge. His teachings were intended for an elect few. His followers started with no authority structure, no infallibility, no traditions, no rituals, no superstitions, but every evolving body throughout history eventually divides and becomes more complicated with time.

Nearly 1,000 years after Buddha died, a new reform

took place. A Buddhist monk in China reacted against his particular training and began a new simplification of Buddhism. The monk's name was Bodhidharma, and Ch'an was the Chinese name of his system. In Japan it was called Zen.

Zen Buddhism

Zen is a technique, or method, by which a person can attain union with the ultimate one. It rejects all the elaborate discipline which the monks put into Buddhism through the centuries, and aims at the center of the target without elaborate ritual or preparation. The idea is simple enough. Since revelation, or inner illumination, comes not by tedious strivings but by a sudden spontaneous intuition, "like a light turning on," monastic traditions are useless.

Many rituals and regulations had grown around the simple teachings of Buddha. Bodhidharma began to teach his own system for attaining the final goal of life. His movement is anti-intellectual and anti-theoretical, striving once again for the purest, simplest path to God. To understand Zen, one must simply be exposed to a few of the *koans*, or riddles, which present insoluble problems for the purpose of shocking, or catapulting, the student into a new level of awareness. For instance, the master points to a flag waving in the breeze and asks his student, "What is moving, the flag or the wind?" Keep in mind there is no pat answer for any *koan*; the student must discover an answer for himself. The answer of the student might be, "Neither, for both are merely in the mind."

Another: "What is the Buddha?" The student

answers, "Two-pounds of flax." It is a way of saying that the question itself is absurd, unanswerable; it is a way of remaining detached from the mystery while being immersed in it.

The Zen Buddhist is not on a trip from life; he wants above all to enter deeply into ordinary human existence; monasticism and all its mysterious traditions are cast aside. He believes he will find truth in ordinary life all about him, and not in the esoteric experiences of mystic teachers. Each must discover truth within himself. The teacher merely guides one to the awakening.

"What is enlightenment?" asks the pupil. "Usual life is enlightenment," replies the master.

In meditation the follower of Zen takes a sitting position with legs crossed and the soles of the feet pointing up. The eyes are half-closed, the hands are in a receiving position at rest before him. The lotus seat position is the one attributed to Buddha when he was enlightened under the Bo tree. It is an attempt to go back to the purity of Buddha's own experience. The meditator empties himself of all thought, memories and imaginations.

The Zen master teaches the message of Zen. A student graduates after mastering about 50 *koan* problems. The *koans* excite an intense seeking for truth. For those interested in studying Zen it might be well to realize at the outset that a full course of training takes about 30 years.

The Practices of Modern Buddhism

Zen is basically a mystery, something which cannot be easily grasped or explained. It is a technique, or method, by which a person can attain union with the ultimate one. But the technique itself cannot be spelled out in words. Consequently, it can only be learned through training sessions with an experienced instructor who leads rather than informs or instructs. Zen must be discovered by means of an illumination of the mind.

You might find it helpful reading some of the sacred writings of Zen to get an idea of the direction of its philosophy. The following is from Zen Patriarch Yoka.

Since I found the path to truth
I am certain that one should not esteem
life or death.

Walking is Zen,
Sitting is also Zen.

If I speak I am silent,
If I rest I hasten:

In essence everything is
The immovable, original one.

If I am threatened by spear and sword,
I never blink an eyelash.

If poison sneaks toward me,
I am not afraid.

How often have I been reborn,
How often did I die again!

Incessant and immeasurable
Life and death lasted.

Yet since I, like a flash of lightning,
Experience the highest truth
I care no more about good or bad fortune.

The oldest Zen poem conveys a similar spirit of peaceful resignation to all experience, taking each thing as it comes without fuss, without distress.

The perfect way is without difficulty.
Save that it avoids picking and choosing
Only when you stop liking and disliking
Will all be clearly understood.
A split hair's difference,
And heaven and earth are set apart!
If you want to get the plain truth,
Be not concerned with right and wrong.
The conflict between right and wrong
Is the sickness of the mind.

Another short Zenrin poem appropriate for the season:

Sitting quietly, doing nothing,
Spring comes and the grass
grows by itself.

Finally, a poem that sums up life as simply as could ever be done:

We eat, sleep and get up;
This is our world;
All we have to do after that
Is to die.

Actually, Zen is a course of self-enlightenment which is independent of written texts. The above poems are merely outpourings of Zen philosophers who have acquired the right spirit. Enlightenment is not transferred through reading, but rather through the sudden flash of illumination which comes from the realization of a new truth. A Zen student might sit for days with legs crossed, the soles of his feet turned up and his hands open before him. He empties himself of all sense experience, opening himself to what Westerners might call "mystical illumination." He knows that God communicates with man in ways other than through sense experience. It is the Buddhist way of prayer: to be still and listen to the movement of God within the depths of his own being, and to search.

The discipline and zeal with which the Buddhist pursues his goal of union with God is most admirable. We can all learn something from the dedication of the devout Buddhist.

Questions to think about

1. How was the "conversion" of Prince Gautama like that of Abraham or Mohammed?

2. What are "selfish desires"? Can you list some? Is it possible to eliminate them? If so, what is left when all "selfish desires" are gone?

3. What is the connection between one's physical position and prayer? What is the value of the lotus position for the Buddhist, prostration for the Muslim, kneeling for the Christian?

THE RELIGIONS OF THE FAR EAST: CONFUCIANISM, TAOISM, SHINTOISM

China's Religious Heritages

China is much in the news lately but there is little mentioned of her three principal religions: Confucianism, Taoism and Buddhism. Since Buddhism was treated in the preceding chapter, we will focus here on China's more ancient religious heritage, Confucianism and Taoism.

China is still so foreign to Westerners that it is difficult for us to assess the present condition of the ancient Chinese religious culture. The so-called "unchanging East" is still in turmoil. The apparent calm surface of Mao's Communist China a few years back broke into volcanic disruption with the fanatical activity of the Red Guard. China today is in the throes of a new swing toward capitalism. Future tremors of shocking magnitude might still be in store for China; we do not know. Yet we do know this: ancient China's influence cannot and will not be erased in one stroke.

While it is true that China is a communist country, the archaic ideas of Confucianism, Taoism and Buddhism still represent a religious heritage of twenty-five centuries. This cannot be ripped from the conscious and subconscious lives of more than a billion people in a few decades. In fact, ancient China is providing the basis for the new China.

Like communism itself, the ancient religions are more concerned with man's well-being than with religious worship, as such. In spite of the many differences found in China's traditions, it is characteristic for the Chinese to harmonize opposites, making them compatible and complementary. In past centuries the majority of the Chinese people were quite comfortable taking bits and pieces from each tradition, molding their own personal religious life as it suited them. All of this was interlaced with primitive forms of worship.

The earliest religious beliefs of China were animistic. For centuries, the sun and moon, the trees and winds, the birds and animals were all venerated as possessing spirits. Ancestor-worship grew out of this mentality, for they believe our spirits live on even after death. Reverence for deceased ancestors no doubt explains to some extent the emphasis in the teachings of Confucious on respect for elders.

For centuries the Chinese were ruled by emperors who were seen as high priests invested by the gods with extraordinary powers. This perhaps explains the phenomenal exaltation of Mao Tse-tung during his rule of China. The Chinese, like the Egyptians, have tended to divinize their monarchs. They also have a neat way of dismissing the ones they dislike.

Monotheism began in the Shang Dynasty (1700 to

1100 B.C.) when a belief developed in a supreme being called Shang-Ti. However this did not mean that the traditional polytheistic gods were rejected. The emperors simply focused greater emphasis on Shang-Ti as supreme. Later, with the Chou dynasty, a shift took place and more reverence was paid to an impersonal god called Tien. The Chou emperors then avoided any reference to Shang-Ti. The emperors of subsequent dynasties became the high priests of Tien with exclusive right to offer sacrifices to heaven. The great Altar of Heaven was built at Peking during the Ming Dynasty (17th Century A.D.) and imperial sacrifices to the gods continued in the forbidden city until the birth of the Republic of China in 1911.

Prior to this the country was one huge feudal system. The emperor alone worshiped the highest God; the princes were responsible for venerating lesser cosmic deities, and the feudal lords and governors prayed to minor spirits. All of these gods supported all the injustices of the feudal system. The rejection of divine worship in China today is not at all unrelated to the rejection of a corrupt feudal system, and the exploitation of the people by rulers who used religion to subjugate them.

Confucius

In 551 B.C., before Socrates was to pioneer an era of philosophical inquiry in ancient Greece, and about the same time that Prince Guatama (the Buddha) began his reform of Hinduism in India, Confucius was born in the Province of Shantung, China. His father, Kung Shu-Liang Ho, a 70-year-old member of the lesser nobility, married a fifteen-year-old girl; their only child was called Kung-Fu-Tzu, or "Kung the Teacher." The latinized version of his name was Confucius.

To understand Kung's writings one must appreciate the situation in which he lived. In 500 B.C. China was in turmoil. The Chou Dynasty was all but finished, and domestic wars were raging as feudal lords drove their armies to butcher one another. Thousands of lives were ruthlessly taken in this futile violence. The desire for law and order is never so strong as in a state of chaos. Out of the rubble China's first absolute emperor was to emerge, but the price of this new rule was heavy. Many of the landed gentry, nobles, artists and intellectuals were thrown out of favor and out of power.

Confucius was one of the displaced persons. He was not a wealthy man, but he was an intellectual who found himself without recognition or position. He wanted a secure and peaceful society. He had begun serious study around the age of fifteen and became an expert in Chinese history and tradition by his early twenties. He loved tradition. He was conservative, respectful of authority, and nostalgic for the idealized, purified forms of the past. In fact his whole ethical system, which he believed God sent him to teach, was basically a revival of feudalism in a stricter, nobler and more purified form.

Although he began working as a low-level civil servant, Confucius felt a strong desire to become a teacher, and so he did, for many years. But at the age of fifty he entered government to become the mayor of a city. From that position he was elevated to Minister of Justice in the principality of Lu. His success was phenomenal in that he brought about a change of manners in the people. The men of Lu acted with honesty; the women were chaste and obedient. As

Confucius grew in wisdom, his fame spread, attracting many students all over China. His standards were always high, so he accepted only an elite group of intellectually ambitious disciples.

> *"To him who has no enthusiasm I shall not open up the truth."*

He believed that wise men should bring their wisdom to the marketplace for the instruction of rulers and for the ultimate good of society. However, he was never given the recognition for which he hoped.

> *"No intelligent ruler arises to take me as his master . . . my time has come to die."*

He died in the year 479 B.C., leaving behind a legacy of writings that have influenced Chinese thinking for 2500 years. But his message was not immediately accepted.

The Legacy of Confucius

Around 255 B.C., China was united for the first time under the Chin Dynasty. The new aristocracy accused the scholars of Confucianism of being reactionary disciples of the past, out to discredit the new order. This was a period of great persecution; Confucianism was banned and nearly 500 scholars were put to death. During this period Taoism began to grow in influence, but time changes everything. By 141 B.C., the new Han Dynasty lifted the ban and Emperor Wu Ti established Confucianism as a state cult. Later it developed into a religion with priests, temples and ceremonies.

Sacrifices were offered at the tomb of Confucius and thereafter emperors competed with their predecessors in honoring the famous philosopher.

Confucius did not claim to found a new religion; his teachings are primarily ethical. He was never revered by his early followers as anything but their "Foremost Teacher." His teaching was simply a system of ethics super-added to the existing religious culture of the times. There was already in his time faith in the supreme deity, Tien. Confucius accepted this tradition and encouraged the worship of Tien, the supreme ruler of the universe, who is often referred to in his writings as "Heaven."

> *"Heaven is the only Great One."*

> *"I have heard that life and death are allotted, that wealth and honors are in Heaven's hand . . . from Him the wise man receives his wisdom, the good man his virtue."*

In the *Aphorisms of Confucius* under the heading "The Emotional and Artistic Life of Confucius," we read:

> *What Confucius took very seriously were: The ceremonial bath before religious worship, war and sickness.*

> *Someone asked Confucius about the meaning of the Grand Sacrifice to the Imperial Ancestors, and Confucius said: "I don't know. One who knows the meaning of the Grand Sacrifice would*

be able to rule the world as easily as pointing a finger at the palm."

When Confucius offered sacrifice to his ancestors, he felt as if his ancestors were present bodily, and when he offered sacrifice to the other gods, he felt as if the gods were present bodily. Confucius said, "If I don't offer sacrifice by being personally present, it is as if I didn't sacrifice at all."

Mangum Chia asked, "Why do people say that it is better to get on good terms with the kitchen god than with the god of the southwestern corner of the house?" Confucius replied, "Nonsense, if you have committed sins against Heaven, you haven't got a god to pray to."

Rsekung wanted to do away with the ceremony of sacrificing the lamb in winter. Confucius said, "Ah Sze, you love the lamb, but I love the institution."

Confucius said, "Respect the heavenly and earthly spirits and keep them at a distance."

It is often said that Confucius had little interest in God, and to some extent this is true, but only partially true. While Confucius was not primarily concerned with religion in his writings, obviously he was a religious man. He was also interested in improving society, in rebuilding the moral climate of civilization; this was the purpose of his writing. Religion was the substructure of his whole philosophy.

Law and Order

The core of his ethical system is expressed in Chinese by the word *li*, which basically means law and order. Confucius says:

> "The principles of li and righteousness serve as the principles of social discipline. By means of these principles people try to maintain the official status of rulers and subjects, to teach the parents and children and elder brothers and younger brothers and husbands and wives to live in harmony, to establish social institutions . . . Through this principle of rational social order (li) everything becomes right in the family, the state and the world."

He idealized the notion of the correct man, or the gentleman, and every act of every person was weighed against what might be expected of the gentleman. Confucius set about to explain how man should act in all his private, family and public relationships. The afterlife was not his concern. "Till we know about the living, how are we to know about the dead?" He concentrated on the immediate relationship of the family.

> *"It is not possible for a man to teach others who cannot teach his own family, for from loving examples of one family, the whole of society becomes loving; while from the ambition and perverseness of one man, the whole state may be led to rebellion and disorders. Such is the nature of influence."*

Two great teachers of Confucianism succeeded the Master in later years: Meng K'o (known to Westerners as Mencius) and Hsun Tzu. Both men believed firmly in the need for education and social formation but they took different approaches to the problem.

Mencius believed that man was basically good in spirit. He attributed the presence of evil to ignorance and claimed that ignorance came about because of a lack of proper training and example. He upheld the importance of maintaining a childlike spirit because the child is naturally good. Hsun Tzu disagreed with him. He claimed that man was naturally evil, children included, and that it was (*li*) training and discipline which overcomes evil.

Chu Hsi, the Thomas Aquinas of Confucianism, did not appear until 1130 to 1200 A.D. In his system of thought he worked to synthesize the best of Buddhism and Taoism into Confucianism.

All three men took pains to purge Confucianism of all religious elements. Confucius says: "Let us leave the heavens to the angels and the sparrows." Right order here and now is the theme.

In his book, "My Country and My People," Lin Yutang, the famous Chinese philosopher, wrote the following description of the spirit of Chinese people, a spirit which was captured and transmitted by the teachings of Confucius:

"For the Chinese the end of life lies neither in life after death, for the idea that we live in order to die, as taught by Christianity, is incomprehensible; nor in the satisfaction of accomplilshment, for that is too vainglorious; nor yet in progress for progress sake, for that is meaningless. The true

end, the Chinese have decided in a singularly clear manner, lies in the enjoyment of a simple life, especially the family life, and in harmonious social relationships. There is no doubt that the Chinese are in love with life, which is so sad and yet so beautiful, and in which moments of happiness are so precious because they are so transient."

Confucius, the Traditionalist

Confucius prided himself not as a creator of new thought, but as a transmitter of ancient Chinese treasures. His great writings are basically a synthesis of the classics of the Chou period (1100 B.C. - 481 B.C.). There are six great works attributed to him:

1. *The Book of Change* (Yi-Ching) — expounds the yin-yang theory. His main thesis concerns the ever-changing circumstances of life, advocating the needs for harmony and balance between yin and yang. It calls for a submission of self to the objective requirements of right order.

2. *The Book of History* (Shu-Ching) — is the story of the great kings of ancient China.

3. *The Book of Odes* (Shu-Ching) — contains the songs and ballads of his times.

4. *The Book of Events* (Ch'un Ch'iu) — contains biographical material on the lives of the rulers of his home Province of Lu.

5. *The Book of Rites* (Li Chi) — contains a listing of ceremonies with commentary upon them.

6. *The Analects* — is a collection of poems and sayings of the Confucius Master. This is his best known book. Before Mao's little red book this was the gospel of China.

Remember these sayings?

Confucius says: If you make a mistake, admit it and mend your ways.

Confucius says: A gentleman sees a question from all sides, without bias.

Confucius says: Goodness is three-sided: in private it is courtesy, in public it is diligence, in relationships it is loyalty.

Confucius says: Never do to others what you would not like them to do to you.

Basically the Master was trying to instill the old feudal code of rites and etiquette into a universal system of ethics for a new age.

For Confucius, morality is not observed out of obedience to divine commands, but rather out of an innate sense of right order. Though the Master thought of himself as one chosen by heaven to teach this correct way of life, he never alluded to any of his precepts as God's will. Right reason and the eternal pursuit of order, harmony and balance are the sole basis of his appeal and his authority. Confucianism, strictly speaking, is not a religion at all — it is an ethical system developed by a social scientist who worshiped his god privately.

Yin-yang

Like the West, China has had a long legacy of myth, legend, rituals and magic. It has gone through centuries of religious evolution, but unlike the West it has tended to organize the whole heritage not around the concept of a single god but around the concept of man. The interplay of forces in human life must be managed and controlled. This is the art of living.

The Chinese spirit must be analyzed in the light of yin-yang if one is to understand the significance of the past or the shape of the future. This ancient formula of Confucianism has deeply penetrated the Chinese view of reality. The power of yin-yang has enabled the Chinese people to ride the waves of history with detachment and dignity.

This outlook underlies all beliefs and traditions, past and present. Yin-yang means that all of life is an eternal interplay between opposing forces: activity and receptivity; male and female; sound and silence; light and darkness; good and evil. Activity and receptivity are signs of interaction which give birth to everything that is. Male is completed by female; sound is completed by hearing; light has no meaning apart from darkness; water has no form without a container. All of these opposites coexist and pursue one another in search of harmony and resolution.

You have probably seen the symbol of yin-yang many times. It is a circle divided by a curved line; one half is all white with a black spot, the other half is all black with a white spot. The meaning of this symbol is both beautiful and profound. The circle expresses the limits of human life. There is opposition within the circle, but harmony is attained without conflict. There is the tension of opposition within the circle, but order exists, balance and harmony are possible. This in effect is the goal of life. They would go so far as to say too much Confucianism is no good; too much Taoism is no good; a little of each is better.

TAOISM

This leads to a discussion of Taoism, for Taoism and Confucianism are deeply related in the Chinese religious experience.

The natural counterbalance to Confucianism was found in Taoism, the second religion of China. The old master Lao Tze (640 B.C. to 524 B.C.) also reacted against the lawlessness and moral chaos of his day, but unlike his younger contemporary, Confucius, Lao was a mystic, not a practical reformer. His teaching was more spiritual than ethical, a teaching not unlike the wisdom of Buddha.

The name "Taoism" (pronounced "dowism") comes from the Chinese word Tao, meaning "path" or "way." The belief of Tao implies an approach to life which is natural, i.e., in harmony with the rest of the universe. A respect for one's own nature, and the nature of things as they are, leads us to the realization that we must pace ourselves in life; we must bend in circumstances in order to survive. Too much haste leads to exhaustion before the task is completed, or worse, causes failure due to poor planning. A sculptor must not strike the stone arbitrarily against the grain, or he will destroy the entire work. The inner nature of things must be studied and respected.

The Faith of the Taoist

Modern Americans are conditioned to interpret a headache as a signal to take an aspirin; for the Taoist it is a sign that he must slow down and let go. The legendary founder of Taoism, Lao-Tze (the Grand Old Teacher), set down the basic principle of Tao, wu wei, which means "let go," "let it happen." It is not a mental health program, but rather a way of life that reaches right up to the ordering of society. The gospel of Tao is entitled *Tao Te Ching*, meaning "The Way and Its Power." Here is an exerpt:

> *A leader is best*
> *When people barely know that*
> *he exists.*
> *. . . Of a good leader, who talks*
> *little,*
> *When his work is done, his aim*
> *fulfilled,*
> *They will say, "We did this*
> *ourselves."*

The philosophy of Tao existed in China a short while before Confucius (c. 500 B.C.) but it eventually became a religion which survived down through the centuries as a counterbalace to Confucianism, which was a heavily legalistic, rule-oriented ethical system. Taoism and Confucianism are like yin-yang, both complement one another. Yin is female — soft and bending (Taoism); yang is male — rigid and rational (Confucianism). The fusion of both has found its way into the Chinese mentality and culture.

Taoism has two forms. One contains elements of sorcery and superstition such as one finds in all primitive religions. The other is a rather esoteric form of mysticism only for an elect few. Each of these are based on the philosophy of intuitive respect for the "natural way life works itself out." It was all started by a human being who was a wise sage. He outlined a philosophy for sensible living, but by the second century A.D., Lao-Tze was worshiped by many as a god. Temples and a priesthood developed around his cult. In China today most Taoist temples are in disuse and the priestly caste is all but extinct.

The gospel of Taoism is a small book of about eighty-one chapters. It is filled with uplifting and inspiring wisdom urging man to empty himself of mundane desires. Much like Buddhism, it points the way to happiness through self-denial. Once the desires of man are extinguished, a state of quiet contentment emerges. This is Taoism, the way. Does it resemble anything you might have seen before?

Qualities of the Taoist

When the highest type of men hear the Tao (truth),
They practice it diligently.

When the mediocre type hear the Tao,
They seem to be aware yet unaware of it.

When the lowest type hear the Tao,
They break into loud laughter —

If it were not laughed at, it would not be Tao.

Therefore there is the established saying:
"Who understands Tao seems dull of comprehension,
Who is advanced in Tao seems to slip backwards;
Who moves on the even Tao (Path) seems to go up and down."

Superior virtue appears like a hollow (valley);
Sheer white appears like tarnished;
Great character appears like insufficient;
Solid character appears like infirm;
Pure worth appears contaminated.

Great space has no corners;
Great talent takes long to mature;
Great music is faintly heard;
Great Form has no contour;
And Tao is hidden without a name.

It is this Tao that is adept at lending (its power)
and bringing fulfillment.

Calm quietude

The highest perfection is like imperfection,
And its use is never impaired.

The greatest abundance seems meagre,
And its use will never fail.

What is most straight appears devious;
The greatest cleverness appears like stupidity;
The greatest eloquence seems like stuttering,

Movement overcomes cold,
(But) keeping still overcomes heat.

Who is calm and quiet becomes the guide for the
universe.

The People's Hearts

The Sage has no decided opinions and feelings,
But regards the people's opinions and feelings as
*   his own.*

The good ones I declare good;
The bad ones I also declare good.
That is the goodness of virtue.

The Sage dwells in the world peacefully,
harmoniously,
The people of the world are brought into
a community of heart,
And the Sage regards them all as his own children.

Although Confucianism and Taoism went through centuries of conflict between their scholars, the two systems have seemed to merge in the course of time.

The Prayer Life of China

Ancestor worship is still practiced by many Chinese, whether they are Buddhists, Confucians or Taoists, or any combination thereof. Some so-called atheists even practice ancestor worship from time to time. The Chinese have this unusually strong sense of family solidarity extending beyond the grave to include deceased ancestors. For centuries most homes have had little shrines with mementos of the families' forefathers who are honored much in the same way that saints are venerated in Catholicism.

The families themselves are clustered in clans and a strong loyalty exists between them. A clan may build its own ancestral shrine for all family members with the same name. These shrines compete with one another in splendor. They contain scrolls of the names of ancient ancestors; and ceremonies are conducted when a new member has died and is added to the scrolls.

There are still festivals and feasts which are celebrated in and around the clan shrines, and special prayers on these occasions are offered seeking the help and protection of deceased loved ones. But the state disapproves of religion and refers to it as superstition. In the major cities, religious ceremonies are rare today and usually held privately or in temples.

Confucius did not devote himself to any study of heaven, but he knew religious feeling helped to stabilize family unity and he was in favor of any influence which supported the family, the basic unit of the social structure.

In the days of the feudal system, feudal lords were expected to offer a particular form of worship to the spirits of the hills and streams. If someone of lesser nobility offered such a sacrifice it was believed the gods would be offended. For centuries, a definite graded system of ritual and worship existed, and it was served by the priestly castes of varying degrees of dignity. The ritual worship of the Chinese has always been family oriented.

China Today

Today things are very different. Communist China is officially atheistic. The spirits of ancestors as objects of worship is debunked. Mao Tze-tung once said: "I hated Confucianism from the age of eight." Shrines are falling more and more into disuse. Foreign religions are scorned, and are barely tolerated only so long as they serve the goals of the communist state. The Red Guard revolution in the '60s included a violent reaction against the practice of honoring elders. Newspapers printed pictures of old men and women having their heads shaved in public by Red Guard teenage mobs. This humiliation was intended to demonstrate the new freedom in China, a kind of liberation from ancient traditions such as Confucianism.

That period is looked upon today as a nightmare. On a recent trip to China I learned that in one city alone there were 52 suicides in one day in June, 1983; all were former members of the Red Guard, the ones who persecuted their elders. The Chinese want to forget their recent past. The old ways however do not die so easily. The passion of new movements tends to wane while the character of a people tends to remain constant. Yin-yang is the spirit of China. The harsh regimentation and cold uniformity of Mao held sway for a while. A balance is being achieved; the pendulum is swinging back. Such is the Chinese spirit, such is the law of yin-yang.

Strangely enough the West has its own yin-yang. The cold war thaw has begun. The inevitability of coexistence with the communist block is being played out in China. We are liable to see a new form of capitalism emerge in a communist state, but it will be a capitalism distinctly different from our own. All this has brought about a complete change in East-West relations which are still being tested.

Even the Church of Rome has changed, vis-a-vis communism. On April 18, 1973, the Vatican made a public overture for a "dialogue with Peking on the basis of Roman Catholic recognition that much of the thought of Chairman Mao Tse-tung also reflected Christian values." The Sacred Congregation for the Evangelization of Peoples, the Vatican's missionary department, issued the statement that Maoist doctrine "contains some directives that are in keeping with the great moral principles of the millenary Chinese civilization and find authentic and complete expression in modern social Christian teaching."

This was a major concession in view of the past experience of relations between China and the Vatican. Those who now search for common ground find in the new regime a rich field in the wisdom of modern China. These more recent developments in world relations are already leading to an era of less tension and more harmony. China seems to have accepted the inevitability of a changing tide. The ebb and flow of life is merely another aspect of yin-yang. No one knows exactly where it will all lead.

Japan's Heritage: Shintoism

Although Buddhism is found all over Japan, the national religion of Japan is Shinto. There are over 95 million Japanese people, and it is esimated that 70 million of these are adherents of Shinto. There is a vast and complicated history to this religion intimately tied into the political history of Japan.

It was traditionally held that two gods created the world and gave birth to a sun goddess who is the ancestor of the mikado, or emperor. The divinity of the emperor was once the heart of the national character of Japan. In the 18th century there was a religious purging in which foreign elements such as

Buddhism and Confucianism were expelled. Shinto was declared the only true religion and faith in the emperor's divine descent was reinforced.

In 1867 Shinto became the religion of the state and was placed under the jurisdiction of the Department of Interior. As such the religion became an instrument of promoting patriotism and national loyalty. Other religions were tolerated, but in all cases the supreme authority of the state had to be acknowledged. The state shrines dedicated to the worship of twelve emperors had to be visited.

Post-War II Japan

In 1946, after World War II, the Emperor of Japan, subservient to the Allied military rule, renounced the myth of his divinity. Shinto was then disestablished as the state religion. Among many of the Japanese, the loss of the war was regarded as the defeat of the Shinto gods.

Many changes have taken place since then. A wide plurality of Shinto sects has emerged, many of them fashioned after Western sects. Monotheism has been proclaimed and the polytheism of Shinto rejected. Today all kinds of religious experience can be found under the Shinto umbrella, from sensitivity groups to faith healers. Since the state no longer controls religion, the people are free to follow any bent they choose.

The Shinto religion has an organized priesthood which is hereditary. Religious aspirations mainly of gratitude and love are ritualized in celebrations of joy. The shrines are usually small, not like Christian churches. They are dwellings of the gods, not assembly halls. Over 100,000 such dwellings, or shrines, still exist in Japan.

A worshiper approaches the entrance through a wooden gateway made of two posts topped by a slightly curved crossbeam which projects on each side, a familiar site in tourist books. Public rituals are conducted at fixed times. The Gods are appeased, spirits are calmed and good will is invoked. The primitive roots of fear and superstition are very evident; however, there are no moral precepts, no commandments. Worship and morality are two distinct things.

Shinto is a subdued religion which makes very few demands of its adherents. Immorality is looked upon as simply the natural state of things. There is an awakening of the female liberation movement which is beginning to have a powerful, unsettling effect on the national life of Japan. Until recently Japan has been exclusively a man's world. Women are beginning to catch on to the meaning of human rights and female dignity.

In brief, modern Japan is rapidly becoming Westernized, economically, politically, intellectually and emotionally. Nevertheless, the predominant religion of the West, Christianity, still accounts for less than one percent of the population.

Questions to think about

1. Is the Confucian more interested in behavior or worship? What about the Shintoist? The Muslim? The Christian? What is the connection between religion and morality?

2. Can you point to some examples of yin-yang in your life?

3. Is it possible for you, when confronted with a problem, to face it simply by "letting go" as the Taoist would? Why or why not?

CONCLUSION

I hope this little excursion through the history of world religions has been an enjoyable experience for you. Learning is an adventure which can have a profound influence on the way you live your life. The knowledge of other religions has helped me to deepen my own faith in Jesus Christ, and to see better the commonality of our human longing for God.

It is my prayer that you will go on to study more deeply in this field of knowledge. There is one central goal behind all learning: St. Thomas Aquinas put it simply, "The end of education is contemplation." We were made not only to know God, but to love Him and be happy with Him forever.

May God bless you and protect you. May the Lord be your strength and your joy, and may your desire to know Him lead you one day to the fullness of the joy He has prepared for you.

Father John T. Catoir